Live Rich
Stay Wealthy
TOTAL
RETIREMENT
FREEDOM

By

Ken Himmler

ISBN-10 0692674926

ISBN-13 9780692674925

U.S. Copyright June 2016

Preface

This book is dedicated to hard-working people who have committed their lives to their families, communities, and their own FREEDOM.

The hope is this will not be another financial book you read and put on the shelf to gather dust. I want you to dig in and read this book over and over again until the processes really sink in.

Without truly understanding how to structure a plan a person's future is like a boat without a rudder.

Retirement is not a fixed age or date. Today's concept of retirement has changed and will continue to change as we evolve our thoughts about what it really means.

Our parents and grandparents depended on their company pensions and the Governmental income sources to provide for their older age.

Today, we need to think of ourselves and our money as if on the Titanic. Plan for the iceberg and have more lifeboats than you need. Most people have no plan at all, or take the attitude that they'll never hit an iceberg.

The problem is, as we all continue to live longer, we experience different challenges our parents or grandparents never faced. Now is the time for you to take action to change your destiny. If you don't put your plan together, no one is going to do it for you.

Contents

CHAPTER 1

HOW TO USE THIS BOOK

I've found most books serve as an educational platform for the do-it-yourself person. I rarely find ones which teach how to collaborate and work with someone.

Inside, you'll find two books in one. There's a do-it-yourself section and a how to work with someone section.

The first part will teach you the reasons why people fail. When you're first learning to drive, your objective is to stay in your lane. This skill is so you don't hit other cars or objects. If you can learn why people fail, and know what to stay away from, you'll accomplish what most have not.

In Chapter 4 through 7, I'll teach you about the tools and techniques on how to craft your own plan, if you want to do it all yourself.

If you're a person who wants to find the right coach to create a guided plan, you should jump to Chapter 8 – Finding a Fiduciary Advisor. This will teach you how to prepare and protect yourself if you're going to hire a coach. Once you hire the coach you'll need to read chapter 4-7 to understand if they're doing the right job for you.

WHAT THIS BOOK IS NOT ABOUT

This information will be very different from the mainstream financial books which are written for the person who's struggling to save a dime.

Some authors talk about not spending $3.00 a week on a coffee or a coke so you can save an extra $50,000 over your lifetime.

That to me is absolutely ridiculous. Are they really saying for the rest of my life I mustn't not buy a coffee or a Coke, or I'll be broke?

I wrote this for those who want to think much bigger than that.

Financial freedom is doing the things you want to do when you want to do them. Buying things you want, when you want. Financial freedom is certainly not depriving yourself of life's little luxuries.

With that being said, I'm sure my children will disagree as they've called me the cheapest person they know.

I don't think I'm cheap, but I don't like waste or inefficiency in any part of my life, time, or money. Therefore, I'm not going to harp on how you can be richer by not spending money on something you want.

I will however teach you how not to waste money on taxes, fees, or bad investments.

This will help you understand, to have the luxuries in

life, you'll need to create so much abundance you don't have to worry about money. It will teach you that to create abundance you'll need a plan and to work the plan.

At a young age, I was an avid reader and fell in love with the wisdom of authors.

As I grew older, I learned sometimes people profess they have wisdom, especially if they're selling something. In fact, in many cases they're making more money selling the information than on operating the actual ideas they sell.

I've purchased hundreds of informational programs, CDs, and books — some good, some bad. I've always been interested to see what others are recommending. Why? It's been my job to stay in tune with what my clients were being presented with. I would say close to 95% of these informational sources are BS.

Here are some examples of some of financial information sources that are BS:

1) Real estate seminars and programs that charge you thousands of dollars to take certain actions that may, in some states, be considered illegal. Promises of cash flow and riches without the reality of what it really means to be a landlord, or to operate rental properties, or flip houses. The "get-rich-quick" schemes of flipping, or buying houses for zero down, only pad the pockets of those promoters selling those programs. Think about it, if you have the means to make

millions in real estate by buying for zero down why would you tell anyone about it? You've just created your own competitors.

2) Gold and Silver. I still see commercials about how the world economy is plummeting — and the ONLY asset you should own is GOLD or SILVER.

These promoters pick the most opportunistic slice of time to show you the rise of these commodities. The only people who consistently win are the brokers who buy, sell, or store these metals.

If you follow TRUE WISDOM, you'll follow those who have actually done it — not those selling this mystical ONE KEY to wealth.

Later on in chapters about asset allocation, you'll learn these types of investments which have consistently underperformed the markets and inflation.

Instead of following these circus barker promoters, follow the real successes. People like Warren Buffet are the types of people to follow. Warren has stated he'll not buy something until it shows income. GOLD and SILVER derive their value purely by greed or fear, not income.

3) Trading and Options. You can turn on any financial program and, if you wait ten minutes, you'll find some commercial telling you about a new software or systems that can outguess the markets. This is the same as the ads for the newest ab machine; for only three LOW payments of $19.99, you can have abs like this young model who looks like this after only thirty days. Come on, do the advertisers really think we're that stupid? YES! THEY KNOW WE HUMANS ARE PROGRAMMABLE. We're programmed to find an easier and simpler way to get what we want. This is why you'll see

> **HIMMLER RULE #1 It is easier to be lured by the potential results of success than to fall in love with the work that creates the success.**

some commercials continue to air because people continue to buy these products.

The sad part is those same people who buy the ab machine (and end up turning it into a clothes hanger in their bedroom) are the same ones who consistently lose on their investments.

Think about it this way: there are pension managers, hedge fund managers, mutual fund managers, and large brokerage firms that spend millions of dollars on software, analysts, and researchers. Some of the best management companies have not exceeded an annual average rate of return of 14% per year, even with all this support.

How then, does anyone think they're going to buy some online program or newsletter and consistently gain higher-than-market returns on their money?

In the late 1990s, I remember turning on the TV and watching a documentary on CNBC about how everyone was leaving their jobs to be Day Traders. There were actually storefronts you could rent direct connect terminals to trade.

Three years later, those stores were out of business and the same people were back looking for jobs.

Again, in 2005, I watched the same show on CNBC. They were doing a show on how people were leaving their jobs to be real estate flippers. Three years later, most of these people were in line to file bankruptcy.

> **HIMMLER RULE # 2**
> **THERE ARE NO ABSOLUTE RULES - IT ALWAYS DEPENDS ON YOUR SITUATION**

History will continue to repeat itself over and over again. The big question is:

Will you repeat the same mistakes?

4) Media such as books, audio programs, and video which promote a single **IF/THEN** statement. This statement "If/Then" is an absolute rule, or so the promoters say. These authors will tell you that in no uncertain terms you should ALWAYS TAKE A CERTAIN ACTION. I've read these materials by some of the most famous authors you might

have heard of. Their promises of giving you that ONE KEY is how they sell more products. The sad part is, there is no **ONE KEY.**

It's no different than the empty promise of losing thirty pounds in only five days with this ONE WORKOUT MACHINE.

Here's a short example of the FIX-ALL statements I've read in some of these best-selling books.

1) Don't ever buy permanent insurance; always buy term insurance.
2) Always buy your home because renting is a losing deal.
3) Always pay yourself first.
4) Always pay down your mortgage as fast as you can.
5) All consumer loan debt is bad.
6) Don't ever buy an annuity.
7) Don't ever buy single issue stock and only invest in mutual funds.
8) Only pay cash for a car and don't ever lease.
9) People without a lot of money don't need a living trust.
10) Always invest as much as you can before tax in your IRA and your 401-K.

> **There's no ONE KEY in any part of your life, especially in your retirement plan.**

11) Real Estate is always a good investment because they're not making any more land.

12) You should take the money you spend on coffee and invest it instead.

Your financial life is more like a combination lock. Your combination is different than everyone else's. Imagine that, out of seven billion people, there's not one single other person out there who has the same financial combination as you.

Now you're saying to yourself, "Then how in the heck am I going to figure this out?"

I promise I'll answer this for you. To start, let's discuss the three rules.

You may have heard the three golden rules of real estate: location, location, location.

There are three rules I've coined to achieve a TOTAL RETIREMENT FREEDOM PLAN. Those three rules are **Calculate, Calculate, Calculate**.

I'm going to teach you what it means to Calculate, Calculate, Calculate. You'll learn how to compare all your choices and not make any decisions until you do the calculations.

As long as you understand throughout our time together, I'll make certain assumptions and use certain concepts that may seem like recommendations.

At no time am I ever saying you should do a certain action in absolute terms. What I'm saying is every action you take should be preceded with a calculation to determine the different possible outcomes.

Why should I be able to teach you?

My mother came from a highly-educated family and she herself with a very expensive education. My father also achieved a high level of education by earning his PhD.

From a young age I was told knowledge was power. Yet both of my parents would be considered financial failures.

With all this *education* around me, you might be wondering why I chose a different route. It was quite simple; I looked at my parents, what they went through to get their education and what it cost them. I looked at their financial security and decided I would take a different route.

I knew that in order to succeed I must get specialized education that would enable me to teach others how to succeed financially. The more people I helped succeed, the more I would benefit.

I first started by becoming an expert in insurance and investments and passed nine of the FINRA qualification tests.

Less than 5% of advisors hold this combination of qualifications.

I then proceeded to get Board Certified in Estate

9

Planning and obtained my Certified Annuity Specialist, Certified Fund Specialist, Certified Estate Planner, Certified Retirement Planning Counselor and Certified Tax Specialist Designations. This gave me the specialized knowledge I needed.

Even this level of education still does not produce a qualified financial planner. It's was my belief that if I was going to help thousands of people obtain wealth I had to do it myself in the same ways my clients were going to do it.

This part of my education would pave the path for me to build wealth through real estate, business acquisitions, stock investing, and running businesses.

From a young age, I seemed to fall into opportunities which would provide the lessons which have served me well in both successes and in failures.

In 1985, I was given an opportunity to work for one of the first financial planning firms in the country. To be quite honest, I didn't plan for this but it was the best opportunity a person could be granted.

For the first nine years, I worked for a firm with a terrific team of planners, insurance agents, stock brokers, lawyers and CPAs. The firm was one of the first "true" financial planning firms that looked at all the aspects of how each moving part connected in a person's financial life.

After nine years, I felt it was important to go off on my own. I was able to acquire a stable of clients, comprised of professional athletes, high net worth business owners, and retirees.

In addition to working closely with these clients on their financial plans, I was preparing over 150 tax returns each year.

In 2005, I wrote my first book — LIVE RICH STAY WEALTHY-FOR WOMEN ONLY.

The reason I wrote it was I noticed many of my high net worth male clients died many years before their female partners. The female was left holding the "bag of money" with no idea of what to do with it.

The book did terrific and sold over 25,000 copies in the first two years. Considering most business books sell about 40,000 books over their lifetime, I was very grateful.

This book allowed me the opportunity for speaking engagements, television interviews, and an ongoing radio show.

Over the past thirty-plus years, I've spoken to an estimated five hundred thousand people between public appearances, and private consultation sessions.

I'm not a doctor or a psychologist, but I've been able to pinpoint some of the behavioral habits of the "financially free" people and those in the financial failure category. In this manual of financial success, I'll outline what I've learned not only from experience, but from working with and observing thousands of financial successes and failures.

I'll bet you caught the failures I admitted to earlier. Yes, I've had many failures and I've learned more from those failures than I have from any financial successes.

Some of my biggest blunders haven't been the miscalculation of numbers but the miscalculation of people I've either worked with, or through.

My biggest blunder was in the late '80s. After building a sizable real estate portfolio of both properties I owned and ones I managed, I sold the company and properties to someone I thought I could trust.

Unfortunately, this person had a drug habit which developed due to the stress of working with more than sixty-five rental units. The deal would've allowed me to retire under the age of twenty-five.

One year into the sale, in which I was holding paper, the buyer ended up keeping all the rents. As the renters left, he sold every appliance and fixture, and even sold the copper wiring and piping to satisfy his drug habit.

He was able to do this because he called the mortgage companies and told them he was me. He then changed the addresses of the mortgages into his name.

He was able to get away with it as this was before our privacy laws and rules on identification.

I'll never forget the Sheriff coming to my house at 11 PM and handing me a summons of foreclosure on all my properties.

The portfolio I'd started when I was nineteen years old — the one I'd spent every evening and weekend building — was all gone.

And so was born my first big lesson in finance: "That which cannot be measured and inspected cannot be managed."

This failure was completely my fault. I held the paper and not once in a six-month period did I go and inspect the properties, or talk with the tenants. It was my first and most painful lesson on how to measure and inspect.

Despite my failures, I continued to push boundaries, studying and developing new approaches for success. I worked with the super wealthy and those just making it. And culling from over thirty years of experience, I've been able to develop a process of success that can be repeated by and for you.

The fast food restaurant, McDonald's, created a system which made it into the most successful franchise in the world. The reason it's so profitable is it can be repeated over and over again no matter where it's done.

Living richly isn't only about having financial success and financial freedom, but it's about having something that improves the lives of others. You can only do that if you have free money and free time. If you're bogged down with daily management for paltry pay, you can only help yourself. Is that really how you want to exist?

If, before that last minute you have on this earth you have the opportunity to reflect, what will you look at? Hopefully, you'll reflect on your experiences. Those people you spent time with and how you might have affected others and our environment.

Of all the clients who have passed away that I've had the opportunity to talk to before their last moments, not one of them was proud of their investment returns or had memories of managing their money.

Their memories were of family, friends, and what they did with their TIME. These people, in their last moments, reflected on the values they've been able to pass down to their family or their community.

My goal with you is to teach you a process of how to structure your money and your future so that once done, you can spend time where it's most important.

This process has been worked on for thirty years and has helped thousands of people create a better life.

In turn, they've been able to educate their grandchildren, give more to church or charity, travel and experience life, help those they love and make sure that they make a difference on this earth.

I hope you're able to get the same benefits out of this book from the information that lies ahead.

CHAPTER 2

WHAT DOES TOTAL RETIREMENT

FREEDOM MEAN?

Retirement is a versatile term. It means a lot of different things to a lot of different people. The term itself comes from governmental control.

In 1881, the President of Prussia, Otto von Bismarck, came up with the idea of retirement. Before this, a person would work until they died. It was common for the older people to hand down the physical labor jobs and simply manage those who could still do the labor. There was a culture of respect for the elderly and their wisdom. By 1888, the Socialist Party pressured von Bismarck to create a plan of retirement. At that time, retirement was pegged at age 70; this was at a time in which the average life expectancy of a male was under age 50.

During the industrial revolution and the ensuing unionization of the United States workforce, our culture simply adopted a mentality that age 65 meant retirement.

This was at a time when it was thought that age 65 was old. People also believed that a person of this age was no longer able to contribute to the workforce.

The concept was sold on the premise and the idea of living a leisurely life on your pension, government income, and savings or investments.

For example, when Social Security was created to start at age 65, the life expectancy was only age 63.

When initially established, the plan was to have two workers contribute approximately $30.00 per year to assist the one person retired.

Now it takes two workers paying in at a cost of $15,000 per year to keep that same one person retired.

Today, the life expectancy of a female is nearing 90 years of age. In a recent actuarial table, the insurance company pushed out the age to 120 years for those born after the year 2000.

In the past, retirement was based on living on savings and investments. This was due to one of the biggest bull markets in history, lasting from 1988 to 1999. It also saw the incredible rise of real estate values in the same period. What is different now?

➤ Home equity is at its lowest level in the past thirty years due to higher mortgages and home equity loans.

➤ The average American has the highest per capita, inflation adjusted, debt load in history.

➤ The average American has the lowest per capita, inflation adjusted spendable income since the 1940s.

➤ We're living longer, causing more medical expenses than ever. Estimates are medical expenses will rise at over 12% per year.

In short, if you'd retired in 1988 at the age of 65 and lived to age 78, you would've enjoyed one of the most fruitful times to retire in history.

On the other hand, if you retired in the year 2000 or later, you would've struggled with one of the worst decades of stock returns. The dark news is the next two decades potentially look to be just as bad.

> **To survive we have to adapt.**
>
> We just have to know what to adapt to!

Why, then, are citizens of America, the greatest country in the world, still struggling with retirement?

It has a lot to do with how slow we embrace change.

We now live in a very different economic environment compared to twenty years ago.

What does the retiree have to face in the next two decades?

➤ Interest rates on investments have been paying below inflation since 2007-08.
➤ Real estate has provided less than an inflationary increase measured from 2000 to 2015.
➤ The stock market has provided only marginal returns above inflation since 2008, assuming you were

even in the right asset classes and managed the funds correctly.

> The government now has a massive 19.3 trillion dollars in deficit. This means compared to the year 2000, when we had a balanced budget, now every American has a debt of more than $55,000. This will have to be paid, and it can only be paid by those who "have." This means if you've saved for retirement or you're a high income earner, expect to pay much higher taxes going forward.

> We're living longer. Health care will be one of our largest expenses and risks as we get older. Don't expect the government to help; it's already broke. Obamacare is one of the worst economic poisons to be swallowed by the American people. In 2015 alone the average cost of health care went up by 14% while the average pharmaceutical company made a profit of 24%.

> Wall Street is not regulated any better than before the great crash of 2008. Yet, profits by financial institutions continue to beat the average return of the everyday investor.

Retirement now needs to be thought of differently. Don't think about retirement as the going-away party, get the gold watch and sit on your front porch watching the traffic until you die. Think of the new retirement as FREEDOM.

Let me give you an example of this from an actual client. I'll call this client Hollywood Joe, to hide his identity. Here's an overview of his situation:

He's single, and works in the movie industry. He is involved in some of the largest motion pictures on the silver screen.

When I started working with him he was stressed out and didn't enjoy work. He thought he needed to work another 5-7 years so he could max out his pension and his Social Security. He also believed he'd have to continue to put up with some of the most obnoxious directors in Hollywood.

All this just so he could get to the magical place of "retirement."

What a way to live, not enjoying your work because you think or believe that you HAVE TO!

It took us about three months to compile an actual retirement blueprint. During this time, we created his Wants Budget and his Survival Budget.

We worked on different scenarios, looking at different lifestyles such as one in which he spent $30,000 a year on books and one in which had travel expenses of $50,000 a year.

Hollywood Joe took six months of going through more plans than I've ever made with anyone else.

Finally, he made the decision to move forward and make the necessary changes in his plan to move him towards his goal of FREEDOM.

His goal of FREEDOM was to never work in the movie industry again. Once we had his plan completed and were assured he could retire and never have to go back he retired, or so I thought.

About six months after his plan was put into place, he decided to take another job on a movie.

In the past, when a producer wanted to hire him, he'd take the job out of fear of not getting another one, feeling as though he "had to" take the job.

This time, however, was very different. He initially turned the producers down and said he wasn't interested.

They came back to him and increased their quote (the amount they offer to work on the movie) beyond his normal asking price. He decided to take the job as they agreed to all of his requests.

The movie took about three months to complete. During that time, I was able to communicate with him when he would get a free minute in his 14-hour work days.

I asked how he was doing and he said he was having more fun on this job than he'd had in ten years. He said he truly enjoyed what he was

> **Freedom comes from knowing and having a plan that achieves what you want.**

doing because he knew at any moment he could quit and walk off the job and he'd still have the life ahead of him which would make him happy.

He also said he was no longer worried about the normal stresses towards the end of the production.

He shared that normally about three to four weeks before the end of a shoot, he'd start feeling very stressed. He explained that in the movie business you'd never know when the next job would show up.

He even shared that as he grew older he started getting stressed about four weeks into the shoot because he knew he was going to be stressed in a few weeks as the project neared its end.

Think about it: he was getting stressed out thinking about getting stressed out. That was all gone now.

We created a plan in which 100% of his

> For an Example of how we create a TOTAL RETIREMENT FREEDOM PLAN go to KenHimmler.com/trf

basic lifestyle expenses would be paid for by his pension, his Social Security, and a fixed guaranteed income. The balance of what was not needed was invested in various bonds, stocks, and other investments.

The nice part was he didn't invest in those types of investments before because of the risks and volatility.

Now he was able to invest and not worry about the normal ups or downs. His FREEDOM plan would provide all the income he needed for life, without these other investments.

It was interesting to see the transformation of a person who thought he had to work another five years into a person who now could demand freedom with his life.

Total Freedom is different for everyone.

It's not necessarily a dollar amount.

It's not the size of your house or the car you drive. It may be as simple as being able to meet your basic needs no matter what happens. Keep in mind, it's not always a game of offense, meaning accumulation. Sometimes it's a game of defense. This means protecting your income and your assets from a major healthcare catastrophe, major investment losses, inflation, taxes, and even possible lawsuits.

> **Fear and stress come from not knowing what the future holds, and being at the mercy of others to determine your fate— like a boss you don't like.**

As you will read, there are certain things you can control and certain things you cannot. The center of stress is worrying about those things you have no control over.

What are some of the things that you can control?

1) Set goals and milestones that will create extreme happiness.
2) Lay out a plan to attain those goals.
3) Find the people who've already done it or are experts

in that area. Hire or associate with them.

4) Understand what you can control and what you cannot control. Focus energy on what you can control.

5) Understand your risks and what you can do to mitigate them.

6) Create a plan to measure results, and continually adjust the plan to meet your final goal.

CHAPTER 3

I'm assuming you wanted this book because you're willing to read something that doesn't have a bunch of fluff and would give you real world answers on how to develop a plan for FREEDOM.

Your request for FREEDOM entails a time commitment by you and, most importantly, a commitment to face reality.

The reality I've learned is most people don't treat their finances like a business. They treat them like a hobby. A hobby isn't designed to make money or be profitable. A hobby is a part-time, leisurely activity. A hobby isn't

> **The new definition of retirement is TOTAL FREEDOM.**

designed to support you, but a business is.

If we face the reality our finances should be looked at like a business, doesn't it make sense to first figure out the differences between businesses which fail and ones that succeed? Of course it makes sense, so let's start with that.

Why Businesses Fail

Let us assume your personal retirement plan is a company called U-Inc. This company has assets, revenues, and expenses. It has risks and untapped potential. Your U-Inc., like any company, needs management talent to sustain and grow.

The SBA (Small Business Administration) tells us that about 80% of new businesses fail in the first five years. Why is that? The main reason is most businesses don't have a written business plan reviewed by experts for proper calculations and assumptions. Your retirement plan is not much different.

It's not enough to have only a written business plan. You can write a plan, but if all of your assumptions of revenues, expenses, and management are incorrect, the plan is known as the Titanic Plan. It's a great looking boat on the

> **If you fail to plan, you plan to fail.**

outside but without enough lifeboats to save those on board, someone is surely doomed.

If your retirement plan is like a company called U-INC, then you are the CEO.

A CEO is not always the expert in the business they operate. What successful traits should a good CEO possess?

1) Able to create a vision.

25

2) Able to create goals that are reasonable and attainable.
3) Able to find talent to accomplish their goals and meet their vision.
4) Able to find the people or methods which can measure and manage the plan to get to the goals.

If you already have extensive investment, tax, estate planning, and insurance training, then you should be the decision-making person. Those areas in which you have skill sets could be put to use.

On the other hand, if you're an engineer and can create complex spreadsheets, it does not mean you have qualifications in tax or integrated retirement planning techniques.

Look at businesses that fail under the same faulty decision-making process.

Believing that knowledge is expertise is one of your quickest ways to planning failure.

Mary wants to start a restaurant because she loves to cook at home and everyone tells her she's is an amazing cook.

This doesn't mean she's qualified to own and run a restaurant.

For Mary to be successful she needs to tap into a team

26

of experts that have done it before.

Usually an overconfident person fails to see a team of experts will get them to their goals quicker, safer and easier vs. trying to be an expert in every area.

Over the years I've tried to compare the successful people to the people that fail. I've tried to figure out what the successes have done vs. what the failures have done.

Here is the list of the items that I've seen the financial failures continually do:

1) The decision-making process.

Failures usually use a decision-by-consensus process. What is this failure technique? They ask people they know for their opinion. They add up how many people don't like something, or like it. If they get a good enough feeling, then they do it. If the people they ask don't understand the question or they themselves have had past failures, then they don't do it.

What if the reason those people they asked failed was because they used the same failure process?

Decide if it's more important to show everyone how smart you are or is it more important to get to your goal.

It's like asking twenty friends: if you went to college

would you get a good job?

Out of the people you ask, some will have failed and some will have succeeded.

The difference is not because of college but it's because the person did something with their degree. It's also not about their successes or failures as there are many components which go into that.

It's about their desire, their decisions, their motivation, and many other factors. In short, ask only those who have what you want how to get it.

2) Believing that knowledge is power.

Knowledge is not power. Knowledge is an understanding. If you understand how an automobile engine works, it doesn't mean you can build one. Calculations, planned actions, and the understanding of strategy is where true power is.

If knowledge were power, why then are the richest people the ones without PhDs?

It's also a well-known fact money managers under the age of thirty-five have less of a sustained performance record. They technically know as much as their fifty-year-old counterparts but they lack the experience.

3) Believing that professionals who give their opinions and beliefs are the experts.

When a CPA, a lawyer, or a financial planner/advisor

says something in the vein of, *in my opinion, I feel*, or *I believe*, without calculating, they're guessing. Just because someone holds a degree or a license in something does not make them an expert.

I would trust Bill Gates (who dropped out of college) to build my technology company over an MIT Graduate who just has a degree. Steve Jobs, Frank Lloyd Wright, James Cameron, Mark Zuckerberg, Tom Hanks, Harrison Ford, Tiger Woods all dropped out of college. There are many so-called "experts" that hang their credibility on a degree, or certification, but who don't take the effort (or don't know how) to do the calculations — they just guess. They themselves might be highly educated but are financial failures.

Are these the people you really want to be learning from?

Experience does not cut it either. Just because someone has been doing something for a period of time does not mean they

> **If you hire someone to create sustainable, lifetime, guaranteed income, ask them if they have it. If they've not created it for themselves, how will they do it for you?**

know how to do it well.

Find the people who have what you want before you let them tell you what to do.

4) Fear of failure.

Fear of doing something wrong stops many people from achieving. A good CEO still has some fear but handles it differently.

A good CEO asks the right questions.
- o What risks am I taking?
- o If this does not work out, where will I be?
- o If this does work out, where will I be?
- o If it does not work out and/or I change directions, how do I get out?
- o How will this be managed?
- o What are my alternatives?

The good CEO makes comparisons of the risks, the returns and then TAKES ACTION. Sometimes that action is no action but it's calculated and a well thought out decision.

5) Failure to take action.

This is a sad reason for failure since many people have all the resources, people, and tools around them to do so much more. Why not put

> **Not making a decision is still making a decision**

those resources, people, and tools to work to make the world a better place? It's one of the most frustrating parts of what I do.

I see some people for whom we could save hundreds of thousands to millions of dollars in taxes and fees, but they do nothing.

I see people sitting on tons of cash not making a dime in return. They are frozen in a non-decision decision. I say that because not making a decision is still making a decision. It's just a decision to do nothing.

Here is an example: Recently, a friend asked for my help. He's in his sixties and has had about five million dollars sitting in cash since 2008. Now, in 2016, this money has been non-productive for eight years. I asked him why he was sitting in cash. He shared with me that in 2008 he lost millions in the market and didn't want to go through that again.

> **The world cannot improve without people with courage**

I gave him the example that if he took $5,000,000 at an inflation rate of 3% then he would be losing $150,000 a year.

This was based on the fact that his funds are spread out between savings and checking accounts earning virtually nothing.

Over the past six years he has lost $900,000 in spending power by sitting in cash.

His response was he knew he should get this money to work but he really didn't need it. He said he had other income coming in from his work. I asked him if he could give the $900,000 in lost earnings every year to a children's charity, cancer research, his church's building fund, or anything that would make the world a better place.

> **Understand what is under your control and that which is not. Focus on improving what is under your control.**

This same person was very conscious about the environment so I was hoping this would motivate him. I'd been with him before where he picked up a plastic bottle on the street to throw it in the trash.

I asked him why he would not take his potential earning power and give that money to a charity. They could pick up tons of trash with an extra $900,000 by hiring people and buying equipment with that money.

He finally got it, but sometimes it takes someone else shedding a different view on things.

6) Greed and fear.

The greed and fear effect has a devastating effect on people and unfortunately we can't just ignore it — we're all human.

What I've see is when something invested is going up in value everyone wants a piece.

This of course happens after it's already gone up in value.

Then, that same person who bought at the top doesn't want to sell the investment. They think this perfect investment will continue to go up with no ceiling.

When it drops in value they sell it at a loss.

Some people repeat this behavior over and over again until they devastate themselves and possibly ruin their family's financial security.

7) Measure and manage.

People are busier today than they've ever been. Money decisions are more complex than in the past.

With this lack of time and the increased complexity, we must have an automated system in place to measure and manage our money.

When I propose putting in place a system to measure and manage,

That which cannot be measured cannot be managed.

most people think, *I already don't have time and I'm already stressed out, and now he wants me to do one more thing?*

If you were a boat captain and you were leaving Miami, heading to a port in Spain, you don't just leave Miami Harbor, point your boat towards Spain, and hope for the best. You have tools to measure speed, fuel, wind, tides, and storms. You have to make adjustments along the way to stay on track. You have to Calculate, Calculate, Calculate.

Imagine you own a company with four branch offices. In each branch office they sell different products by different people. There's no system in place to know if each branch is profitable or if it is losing money. There's no system in place to know if your employees are making you money or stealing from you. How long do you think you'll stay in business? Not long!

This example is no different than your personal financial or retirement plan. You have four branches: Investments, taxes, asset protection, and insurance. You need a system! An automated system measures and

> To see a live example of how an automated system works, go to kenhimmler.com/trf/mgpautomation

automatically reports back to you how your different branches are doing. The system tells you if there are any issues that need to be fixed, on an automated basis.

In summary, you have a company that has to be run.

How are you going to run it?

Where you start

As we ended the last section, I said we would face all the potential problems and pitfalls first and then create a plan that addresses all the risks and potential problems.

Once we outline each obstacle, we need to understand what we can change and what we cannot change. From this, we will create a realistic plan that will get you to your end goal.

These obstacles are both exterior (economic and mechanic processes) and interior (you, and how you make decisions).

Let's outline each obstacle in priority:
1. Belief systems that prevent change or a different way of getting to a goal.
2. Lack of a written goals with dates and dollar amounts.
3. Lack of a PLAN.
4. Focusing your energy on what you cannot control vs. what you can control.
5. Procrastination.
6. Investment Strategy.
7. Tax Strategy.
8. Protection Strategy.

35

YOU AND YOUR BELIEF SYSTEM WILL CREATE YOUR BEHAVIOR

Einstein once said the only thing harder than an atom to crack was a belief.

We humans are programmable computers. You can decide on your own programming; you own the keyboard. This means your decisions and beliefs will change your financial outcome.

> ➤ What are you doing to improve the way you make decisions?
> ➤ Are you questioning your old belief system?
> ➤ Are you trying to improve YOU along with your retirement plan?

It's important to look at your decision-making process and belief system as these will direct you to success or failure.

Look at how big business uses belief systems to sell you more of their products or services. Big corporations know if they can modify your beliefs, they can modify your behavior. If they can modify your behavior, they can control your buying habits.

Every time we see a product or service commercial, it's designed to program us to modify our beliefs.

If you've visited Las Vegas, you'll see human behavior programming at its best. Lights, action, and noise. All the surroundings of the Las Vegas Strip are designed to get you to part with your money.

Las Vegas spends millions of dollars each year learning how to program humans. Here is a short example of Vegas conditioning:

1) Darkened gambling areas.
2) No clocks on any walls.
3) Swirl colored patterns on the carpets.
4) Double metal coin catchers on slot machines.
Walkways and confusing exits that force you to pass slot machines.

When someone wins, the casino makes noise. This calls attention to the big win. This activates human dopamine which then increases confidence in winning. It is scientifically proven that if you see someone else win the dopamine in your brain increases, thus giving you more tendency to follow what the other person is doing.

Maybe you remember the restaurant Howard Johnson's. In the mid-fifties and sixties, they studied colors and how they would affect moods and hunger. After careful testing, they found a special color combination would trigger the dessert craving. Those colors, the now signature blue and orange colors created hunger for desserts.

Subliminal programing was tried in the 1950s by adding a millisecond commercial throughout movies. These short commercials were so short they were not even noticed by the human eye. Even though your conscious mind did not see them, your unconscious mind did.

These commercials were designed to get you to buy more popcorn and soda. Sales went through the ceiling and the government got worried communists would try to control people's beliefs and idealism with this secret.

Congress was so afraid of the effects they ruled this to be a crime. It became illegal to put any message of this kind into any movie or media.

Does this mean if you see the message you'll be able to judge whether to believe it or not?

Wall Street has proven they can put the message right in our face and humans will still believe it. Look at the way the markets are structured.

> ➤ A bell opens the markets.
> ➤ A bell closes the markets.
> ➤ A ticker shows all day with numbers moving up and down.

This is a human attracting system designed to keep us engaged. If this constant engagement really worked, then why do the most successful investors admit to not watching any of the market's gyrations?

Titans like Warren Buffett, Sir John Templeton, and John Bogel have admitted to not looking at markets for extended periods of time.

Warren Buffet said he focuses on the business aspects of what he owns as the stock market is drama driven.

John Bogel, founder of Vanguard says to "shut your eyes and let the markets do their thing."

Do you think your own behaviors and decisions on how you manage money have gotten you to where you are? You better believe it.

EXPERIENCE

Experience can be a good or a bad teacher. Experience is one of the ways we form our beliefs, which form our behavior, which form how we make decisions. Depending on how you interpret and use the experience can determine your future decisions.

To certain people, if they've had a bad experience then they will never take that action again. I've heard the following from clients:

- I lost a lot in the 1999 and 2008 crashes, and I don't ever want to invest again because I'll lose money.
- I'll never buy rental property again. I lost a lot in the 2009 crash.
- I would never buy an annuity because my golfing buddy said they're terrible. (Here is one in which the person creates a belief system from someone else)
- I would never use a reverse mortgage. Isn't that where they take your home?
- Probate is no problem — I handled my father's estate in three weeks.
- I'm not worried about a long-term care catastrophe,

my mother was only in the home for one year and then died.

- ➢ I gave my money to an advisor and I lost a lot.
- ➢ I don't need any family asset protection. I handled my inheritance wisely and I expect my children will too.

All of these statements are from the person's experience. This does not necessarily mean that the experience will repeat itself.

Have you ever said something similar and learned later that your decision was based on a past experience that did not repeat itself? There might have been other factors that you did not know about at the time of the bad experience that made it a bad experience. A new experience may have a totally different set of circumstances.

EMOTIONAL TIDES

Just like the ocean tides go up and down, people's emotions do the same. The problem is when you add emotion to the logic and math of the financial world, you're asking for disaster.

The day after 9/11 people were not in the mood to rush in and buy investments. There was a huge void in everyone's emotional security about their physical and economic future. On the other hand, at the end of 2014, people wanted to rush to invest in the stock market after two years of stellar returns.

This emotional tide we humans act on has not changed much over the last ten thousand years of civilized history.

I recently dealt with this with a person who tried to hire me. At the time she was 50 years old, single, and making over a million dollars a year. She said she wanted to change her investment strategy and wanted my help.

She had been working with another planner but wanted to change. With this other planner she originally invested $500,000 on her own and originally wanted an aggressive portfolio.

In this type of aggressive portfolio, you should have a one-year period to get fully invested. This is done to reduce the risk. It also would have a ten-year holding period to allow the volatility to average itself out. The original planner had set this strategy up correctly.

Upon interviewing her, I found the initial buys of this new aggressive portfolio were done with only about 40% of the total portfolio and only over a six-month period. The other 60% was still sitting in cash waiting for allocation during this one year buy-in.

During the initial six months the portfolio dropped about 20%. As soon as this happened she went through an emotional tide.

She pulled all the remaining cash out of the portfolio and put it into the bank.

I tried to explain that the 20% drop was the best thing

that could've happened. Now the investment plan of buying in would give her a lower average buy-in price. I told her if she truly intended to hold onto it for ten years, then this should not be an issue. She should actually be trying to scrape together as much cash as she could to buy in more at a 20% discount.

She didn't put the other 60% back into the buy-in strategy and left it in the bank. The plan did not fail, she failed to follow the plan. The original planner had created a solid road map but she strayed off course.

Will she now blame the markets, the advisor, or her own behavior?

What will continue to destroy people's future? Obviously, **making the same mistakes over and over again**.

Many people can recognize other people's mistakes and see no problem judging their neurotic behavior. Yet, they commit the same mistakes over and over again.

The way to TOTAL RETIREMENT FREEDOM is not the "best investment" or the "best strategy." The key is to first improve yourself. This is done by understanding how you make decisions and what drives those decisions.

Forgot all your past beliefs and wipe the slate clean. Remember, you are where you are now because of your decisions. If you want to grow, protect yourself, and be better, then you must follow those who have accomplished what you want. It also means you must change the way you think.

A true assessment of yourself will be a good determinant on how you'll handle your plan going forward.

If you bring these emotional tides into a relationship with a professional planner, you may not be able to keep that relationship. Most top-end planners I know don't keep clients who ride this roller coaster of emotion.

On the other hand, if you're able to truly understand how to structure and manage your financial plan, you'll work better with your professional partner. Even if you're going to do it yourself, understanding the structure and process will allow you to work better with yourself.

This person I just used as an example is a person we decided not to take on as a client.

The next step is to understand your WHY. This will help you understand what to focus on.

LACK OF A WHY (GOALS)

This is my favorite part of working with people. I personally get so fired up helping someone in their forties, fifties, sixties, or even seventies.

It's wonderful to see them reinvent their lives by setting new and meaningful goals.

The problem we have in our school system is we don't teach how to set and achieve financial goals.

This must be why we now see children in their late

twenties and early thirties either still living at home or moving back home.

If you could give your children or grandchildren a single gift what would it be? I would say the best gift to give someone is to teach them how to set, monitor, and achieve their goals. In order to give that gift you must first possess it yourself. You cannot give something you do not have.

In the Hollywood blockbuster movie, *The Truman Show,* they showed what it's like living inside a bubble. What an awakening when a whole new world was found.

Many people will continue to live inside their own bubble of capacity thinking until someone shows them the outside.

Dennis Waitley talks about the Harvard Goal Study. In this study, a group of one hundred Harvard students were asked their goals. About thirty of them had goals, but only three had written goals with a plan. Yes, that is only 3% of Harvard students had written goals.

Twenty years later the study was repeated. The three people that had written goals were by far the most successful. Their income and net worth accounted for 90% of the net worth and income of the original one hundred.

> **HIMMLER RULE # 3
> THE LACK OF A
> CLEARLY DEFINED
> GOAL WILL ASSURE
> FAILURE**

Goals are the motivation to take action. Goals are the

fuel in the tank. Goals are why we do things. You need to outline your goals in detail as this will be your true motivation. Let me first explain what a goal is not;

- A goal is not to improve your investing.
- A goal is not to improve your budgeting.
- A goal is not to insure your life or income.
- A goal is not to protect yourself from lawsuits.
- A goal is not to protect yourself from a health catastrophe.

These are actions or objectives to improve your financial outcome, but they are not goals.
A goal is something that will give you happiness.
An objective is the action to get you there. Once you have a solid list of goals, your next step will be to create a plan. Without a plan, goals are just empty dreams.

LACK OF A PLAN

If you're a good goal setter and have done all the work to lay out what you want, the next step is to develop your plan.

Studies show only 5% of new businesses create a true business plan. Further studies show that less than 10% of people who create a retirement plan, an investment plan, or a diet actually follow through.

45

If you are like me, you love to go and look at houses, both for investment research and to dream-build.

Let's say that you see your dream home but someone already lives in it. You want this home so you're going to build it. Hopefully, you have a picture of every detail of this house in your mind. You can see what it looks like inside and out. You can mentally walk through each room and visualize every part of the house. What's your next step to turn this from a vision to a reality?

HIRE AN ARCHITECT!

I hope you didn't say to start hammering nails. With many people, I've seen them structure their retirement plan this way.

They determine an amount they need each month for their living expenses. They then try to compute the rate of return they have to earn on their investments to obtain this monthly income. Finally, they try to find investments that have that projected or average rate of return.

The problem with this method is as soon as the investment does not meet the returns needed to pay them their monthly expenses, people sell and change the investments.

Sadly, many people make these changes in the first year, whereas these investments should be held for five to ten years. After they lose money they then blame the markets, the government, or the broker that sold them the investments.

A proper plan has staged income payouts from investments over a 1-5 year, 5-10 year, and a 10 year plus strategy. This laddered effect allows a steady income without worry of the volatility of the markets.

The proper method of building your TOTAL RETIREMENT FREEDOM PLAN is not much different than building a house.

You first need to create your vision of what you want to build. You then find the land which will fit the building you want to construct.

Once you find the land, you hire the architect to draw your blueprint. The architect is there to bring your vision to reality. The architect is also there to tell you what is physically possible or not.

If your lot is 50x50, then you may not be able to build a 5000 square foot house on it. It's the architect's job to work within the rules but still meet your goal of what you want.

This is not being negative or limiting in thinking; it's a physical constraint. The lot is what we refer to as your Plan Foundation.

As an example, let's say you're still working and an important value to you is your family. What if your goal is to retire by age sixty, but it means taking a job that would keep you on the road three hundred days a year?

You'll be away from your family, which is your most important value. Would you take this job and break your values to reach your goals? This is where you may have to make some compromises.

If you truly want a bigger house and your lot will not accommodate it, then it's time to find a bigger lot or build a smaller home.

What does this mean in terms of your retirement plan? If your current investment or income production will not get you to your goals, it's time to figure out how to change. You must change either your goals or your investment and/or earning capacity.

WHAT YOU CAN AND CANNOT CONTROL

I am a big believer that people create their own financial futures. If you believe in this, you'll have a much easier time growing, rather than being a victim or having an entitlement mentality.

Financial success is much like losing weight. Experts say that 85% of your diet success is what you put in your mouth and only 15% depends on your exercise or workouts.

It's dependent on you, and how you think and your decisions. This isn't to say there won't be forces out there acting against you, as in the game of Monopoly.

You might roll a bad throw and get hit with a Community Chest penalty.

These losing rolls of the dice are in the uncontrollable

category. No matter what you do, or how you behave, these items will affect you.

You can waste your time complaining and barking about how unfair they are, or you can simply recognize there are uncontrollable events. What are some of these unlucky rolls of the dice?

- Global economics.
- Political changes that affect economics.
- Macroeconomics that affect inflation.
- Trade deficits and currency devaluation.
- Demise of the American quality of healthcare.
- Stock market ups or downs.
- Governmental bailouts.
- Demise of the Social Security and Medicare system.
- Healthcare catastrophe.
- Premature death.
- Changes in Social Security, Medicare, and tax rates.
- Divorce.
- Interest rates.
- Income tax rates and rules.

I could go on, but I'd like to focus our energy on what we *can* control. The best part of your opportunity for financial success is that it depends on you, and you alone. Here's the list of the items that you can control:

WHAT YOU CAN CONTROL

A) Your belief system, personality traits, and how you make decisions are controllable actions.

Financial arrogance, as I will explain it in this context, is when someone thinks they know it all. It's when someone thinks they know better than anyone else and can't take direction, coaching, or advice. Their self-esteem is buried in the facade of wanting people to think they are the smartest person in the room. It's also emotional ties to old cultural concepts. Do you hold onto emotional concepts and lose the benefits of mathematically calculated financial strategies that would benefit you?

> **HIMMLER RULE #4**
> **FINANCIAL ARROGANCE IS THE BIGGEST KILLER OF RETIREMENT SUCCESS.**

B) The Amount You Spend Every Year is Controllable.
Your budget is a belief system that you have built.
Many people learned during the great depression/recession of 2008 they could live on much less than they originally thought. I'm not saying you should create a live-in-a-box - under-a-bridge budget. I'm saying that you should have three budgets:

50

- A Survival Goals Budget
- A Basic Needs Budget
- A Wants Budget.

When you get to the planning stage, test each budget to see what you really can accomplish. It's my belief that if you have a good plan you'll be able to achieve TOTAL FREEDOM, whatever that means to you.

C) The Amount of Investment Risk You Take is Controllable.

Risk is not a subjective opinion; it's a measurable calculation of how a loss can be handled in your personal financial fingerprint.

I continually hear people telling me that their financial advisor has told them they're in a conservative portfolio. After further investigation I almost always find they're in stocks that have history of dropping up to 40% in bear markets. How then does this broker/advisor come up with the statement that they are in a "conservative" portfolio?

- Does it mean it's conservative in comparison to the overall market risk?
- Does it mean in this advisor's "OPINION" it's conservative?
- Does it mean it's "conservative" in

51

comparison to other investors?

Change the words from the nebulous Conservative Portfolio to Sustainable Portfolio.

The only way to know if you have a Sustainable Portfolio is to measure what the largest drop has been in the past against what you can or cannot afford in volatility.

While this measurement is no promise the past will repeat itself you have to have a baseline to start with.

After you know the true downside, you can do the

> If you would like to take a financial personality test you can go to our site (www.kenhimmler.com/trf/personality) and see how your personality and decision making skills compare to the most successful investors.

calculations. If you had to sustain this drop, could you continue to live the same way and accomplish all your goals? I believe if you're able to answer yes to this, you have a Sustainable Portfolio.

On the other hand, if you have to change your lifestyle or you run out of money, I don't care what this advisor says, you don't have a conservative or a sustainable portfolio.

The amounts of risk you take are within your control and it's up to you, or whomever you hire, to measure risk as it applies to you and only you.

I recently had a conversation with a client. In deciding

the client's Asset Allocation Model we determined that they could afford volatility in the portfolio.

From the questions the client asked, I feared he would not be able to psychologically weather any short term volatility in his portfolio.

He asked the question, "Ken, what do you think the direction of the overall global economy and the direction of the stock market for the rest of this year will be?"

> Volatility risk is the amount that an investment swings up or down. This is also known as Standard Deviation

I explained this had NOTHING to do with the selection of his Asset Allocation Model.

He was stuck on thinking he had to out-guess the global economic future. What he missed was that no one can predict or control these economic levers.

What can we learn about this person from his questions?

- Does he understand that an Asset Allocation Model applies to his personal cash flow and not to global economics?

- Does this person understand that asking himself or anyone else for a prediction is a 50/50 loser's game? If he guesses right, or worse, his advisor guesses right, he now has a false sense of prediction capability. If he guesses wrong, he loses, and he may develop a belief system that the stock market will always lose money. If his advisor guesses wrong, then he'll be mad at the advisor. Regardless of the scenario it has nothing to do with a five-to-ten-year portfolio as it applies to his cash flow, his expenses, or his personal lifetime plan.

How do you bridge the gap between understanding what risk you really have and what risk someone might be telling you you have? You have to have a system in place for determining how you gauge risk. Are you going to:

> Determine risk based on the opinion of the advisor?
> Determine risk based on the objective of the mutual fund brochures?
> Determine risk based on what you see on TV?
> Determine risk based on your friend's past successes?
> Determine risk based on what you read on the Internet?
> Determine risk based on the chance of and the amount the investment can drop?
> Determine risk based on how secure you feel at the moment?
> Determine risk based on an independent risk

analysis? This should only be done by a Fiduciary Advisor that does not sell products or work on investment commissions.

To get a third party assessment of your risk go to www.kenhimmler.com/trf/riskassesment You will be able to insert your investments to see what your Standard Deviation or Volatility Risk is

D) You control the distribution system you use.

You determine the system and the methodology of how you set up your distribution system. There are a few ways you can distribute assets and income

There are a few different methods of distribution. Some of these methods are efficient and some are not. The first method, called the Haphazard Method and the subsequent method, called the Scraping Method, are the worst ways to set up your distribution plan. Keep in mind, these are strategies you can control. Let's start with the first method called the Haphazard Plan.

1) The Haphazard Plan. In other words, no plan. You take money from whatever accounts or investments seem convenient or easy. You might even be the Haphazard RMD Person.

This person makes distributions from the retirement plans with no plan in mind. This faulty strategy is to have your cash flow or expenses covered by your RMD.

The problem is your RMDs are not earnings. They are distributions based on a percentage of the account value.

If you have the wrong investment strategy, you might lose 50% inside your IRA.

| RMD stands for Required Minimum Distributions, and are required on all retirement plans to start at age 70.5 |

If you have to take out a fixed percentage based on the prior year's value, you're taking out funds at a loss if you sell any of the underlying investments.

That's not a sustainable distribution method but more of a recipe for disaster.

This Haphazard RMD Person also doesn't consider there are certain assets better taken out than others.

This person usually takes out cash to satisfy the RMDs as opposed to looking at each underlying asset to determine if there are better assets to take. We'll cover this more in the discussion on GAMMA.

2) The Scraping Method. As an example, you might have five different accounts, one CD, one stock dividend-paying account, an annuity, an IRA, and a bond.

How do you get income? This failure method takes the interest from your CD, your dividends from your stock, a monthly income from your annuity, your required minimum distribution from your IRA, and the interest from your bonds.

You add it all up and add your Social Security and pension. This total is how much you figure you can live on in retirement.

This is a Haphazard Method as it doesn't consider taxation, lower-paying investments, or high-risk investment strategies.

It also doesn't consider certain investments need dividends to reinvest to attain their average rates of returns. If the dividends are getting paid out to you for income, there's no risk reduction by the dividends buying more shares when they are down in price.

3) The Calculation Method. This is the only proven methodology of maximizing the distributions.

This is sometimes referred to as the Planned Distribution Method. This is the longer and more mathematical way to calculate, but the more sustainable way to obtain a lifetime income.

It also takes a full understanding of the calculation and the software tools to be able to compute this. It is next to impossible to figure this out from a spreadsheet.

The distribution strategies in this method are:

1) Lowest Taxation First.
2) Highest Liquidity First.
3) Lowest Risk First.
4) Custom Schedule Distribution.

Each combination potential of distribution must be calculated to come up with the most efficient one based on your situation. There are multiple possible orders of distribution and also customized schedules.

With a customized schedule you can change the order of each investment or account that distributes based on your cash flow needs, risks, and tax situation.

I would suggest you go to the video explanation at www.kenhimmler.com/trf/distribution. This can show you the benefit of having a planned and calculated distribution method.

Will this really add any net benefit to you? In an article written by Morningstar they termed this distribution method as GAMMA. This particular report estimates that additional planning and a distribution strategy can add as much as a **29%** increase to your retirement net income. This equates to

You can go to www.kenhimmler.com/trf/distribution to learn more

a **1.82%** potential increase in your net return.

There are people searching under every rock and crevice for investments that will earn a better rate of return.

It's not always a better investment that will improve your plan. It might just be a different distribution method.

Why go out to try to get a better rate of return by investing in something riskier? What if you could invest in something safer but simply net a better rate of return? You are earning more with less risk. Isn't that the end result we are all looking for?

Do you remember your first job? Were you excited to get your first paycheck? If you're like me, you were quite surprised when you actually got the paycheck and looked at your real take-home pay.

I remember looking at my pay stub and asking where the heck did the other 40% of my earnings go?

It's not any different in your investment strategy. You can strive for the highest returns but you have to take the risk.

Alternatively, you can strive for a lower risk but a higher take-home paycheck. Which sounds more reasonable to you?

No matter where you're at now in your financial life you'll need to either update your plan or start one to figure this out.

It's been

> **A good financial planner will attempt to identify problems and behaviors before making any recommendations.**

truly amazing to watch human nature at work. There are some people who create a plan and follow it to the smallest detail. Then, there are those who create a plan but continue to revert to their old learned behavior of fear, greed, and making decisions by consensus. Let me give you two examples of this.

The first case is a single man who I'll call Charles. Charles is 60 years old, single, and owns a corporate consulting business. He goes into companies and solves problems between the companies and the employees. Charles was netting about $350,000 in annual income. He had accumulated about $1,000,000 in net invested assets.

If you're a financial planner for a long period of time you can tell which people are going to present a potential behavioral issue to their own future.

This instinct comes from interviewing skills and simple math. At age sixty, with $350,000 of earnings a year and only $1,000,0000 accumulated, there's a problem.

Unfortunately, even the best of financial planners cannot always change someone's decision-making process.

> *Only 10% of people follow through with a retirement plan, a financial plan, an investment plan, a business plan or their DIET!*

The problems I've seen are:

➢ Making bad investment decisions due to lack of calculations.
➢ Fear of making bad decisions and not investing any money.
➢ Greed and Fear. When investments go up, they buy and as soon as they go down they sell, continually losing money.
➢ Spending too much money.
➢ They are too busy to oversee things and someone they hired is stealing money. We find this frequently with professional athletes and entertainers and physicians.
➢ Giving money to family, friends, or anyone who shows up on the doorstep looking for a handout.

In Charles's case, it looked as though he had most of these problems.

Charles's goal was to retire in five years. We worked very hard to create a plan that was calculated down to the smallest action which would allow this.

His income goal was to be able to spend the same amount of income he was accustomed to while he was working.

In addition to his income goal, he wanted to move out of a high-tax state, California, to a no-tax state, Florida. While this isn't for everyone, his personal goal was to be closer to family.

After our analysis, we found he didn't need to wait the five years. We could reconfigure his plan to allow him to reach his goal in only one year.

With this new-found knowledge we put into place action items that would allow this to happen.

Unfortunately, because of his procrastination, it took him two years to implement some of the actions which could have taken him only a month to put into place.

This procrastination delayed his goal by two years. After two years of prodding him to take action he called to tell me he was going to change his entire plan because he had met a guy in Mexico. He was going to partner with this guy on a technology venture.

He just met this person but he changed his entire plan to take his money and invest in this new venture.

I asked him some of the hard due diligence questions about this "wonderful" deal he thought was the jackpot. He couldn't answer any of the questions. He kept going back to "this could make me millions overnight."

Charles was a Harvard graduate but it didn't improve his bad financial decision-making behavior.

Just because someone has an Ivy League degree does not mean it will change their beliefs or behaviors.

If you're going to do this alone, without a planner or coach, you have to recognize your weaknesses. If you're on a diet you don't want to keep cookies and sweets in your house. Overcome your weaknesses by creating systems and processes which will help you take emotions out of the decision making process.

I want to use another example of a person who had similar education, status, and goals. The next client I am about to tell you about came to me only one year after Charles.

I'll call him Bob. Bob had been an insurance company executive. He had run a large investment and business department at one of the country's largest insurance companies. His goal was to retire in one year and never go back to work. We talked about taxes, income, expenses, and the entire calculation methodology.

We created a detailed plan which Bob participated in every step of the way. Bob spent a considerable amount of time as a good CEO working on his plan. He spent 90% of his time developing his three budgets. His Absolute Need Budget, his Baseline Budget, and his Dream (or Wants) Budget were thought out with great care.

The discussions were fun and light. His wife kept teasing him about the budgets to make sure he wasn't putting a sixty-inch TV in every room.

As a planner, it was one of those enjoyable cases. I could collaborate with them to obtain a desired goal. What more could a financial planner ask for in job satisfaction?

Their plan was to move to a non-taxed, low cost of living state. Bob and his wife took trips to Florida, Nevada, and Texas. They decided they would land in Texas and they began the hunt for the right house.

Each step of the way Bob would email me and give me different houses to run though the calculations to determine which ones would work within their plan.

They finally decided on the right house for them. They had the right plan in place and they made that big jump into retirement.

The last I've heard is they're still living in Texas and compromised on the sixty-inch TVs. (There are only a few.)

The reason I want to highlight this client is he had experience in being an executive so it was easier for him to act the part of the dream weaver. He provided the vision, then collaborated with the experts to get him where he wanted to go.

Here are two equally educated people, earning about the same income. One has accomplished his goals and keeps his plan on course.

The other continues to exhibit the same failure behavior over and over again, getting the same results: financial destruction.

This may not be what you wanted to hear, but it's the TRUTH.

KNOWLEDGE IS NOT POWER. It's the collective knowledge of many people put into a coordinated plan with vision and acted upon which is power.

The good news is you can control how you put your TOTAL RETIREMENT FREEDOM PLAN together.

Even though you do have control and you may have the CEO mentality, you may still have a challenge in delaying your success. This may be because this is a whole new way of operating.

PROCRASTINATION

The world is full of failures. Failures constantly state that they "don't have the time." I think it's more prioritization of time rather than a lack of time.

Have you blamed the procrastination of making financial decisions on a lack of time? Have you failed to complete the fundamental actions to get to your goals? Procrastination will cost you in dollars. Here is an example:

One of our clients was a Hollywood producer with one of the longest running television shows. He's what I would call the King of Procrastination.

While in his early sixties, he was still sitting on over $6,000,000 in cash parked in money markets earning less than 1%. We constantly tried to get him to put this money to work but his excuse was always, "I'm too busy at work."

Maybe my mind thinks differently, but I look at that as an expense — leaving these funds parked at about $15,000 every month.

Here is how this is computed:

$6,000,000 in accounts.

$60,000 currently being earned at **1%** rate of return.
If all he did was to invest this money at a conservative bond
rate of **4%** then he would have.

<u>**$240,000**</u> in total earnings.

If we subtracted the current earnings of **$60,000,** then
he has **$180,000 a year in lost earnings** or **$15,000 a month
in lost earnings**.

To break it down even further, he is losing $3,500 a
week.

At a daily level he is losing $500.00 a day!

I know what you're thinking —, *sure, if I had
$6,000,000 I wouldn't do that.* Really, are you sure? I find
people either manage well or poorly no matter how much
money they have. It's a personality and motivational pattern
of a person.

Look at the failures that plague lottery winners. More
than 80% are broke after only four years. Why is that? If they
couldn't manage a small amount of money they can't
manage a large amount.

I'm assuming you are motivated enough to do

something to improve your financial situation. If so, let's look at yet another mistake that people make— their investment strategy.

INVESTMENT STRATEGY MISTAKES

An investment strategy mistake is a common mistake people make. Part of people's failures are seated in Wall Street's ability to make investing confusing. I believe most of this confusion-manufacturing is intentional.

Investment choices can span from stocks, bonds, mutual funds, real estate, REITs, private equity, and even annuities. The question I always get is: "Which is better?" It all depends on what you're trying to achieve, the time period until the money is needed, and your personality.

In the short term, investments go up and down depending on global macroeconomics, national economics, daily news, and investor sentiment.

In the long term, investments go up based on birth rates, free spendable income per person, profitability of companies, and government taxation.

Market emotion plays less of a part of your returns over the long term. Long term, is no shorter than five years but on average is more around ten years.

How do you determine which investments, categories or classes will go up or down at any time? Can you or any computer program make any reasonable predictions? Let's use a science project to answer this.

Have you ever seen a wave motion machine? Sometimes people call them gravitation machines. These are desk ornaments which are about a foot long, formed in a glass or acrylic block.

Inside is water or a thicker solution such as they use in lava lamps.

When you push one side down the water or solution fills to that side. When one side fills, the motion and energy pushes the water to the other side. Once you push the one end down, the ongoing motion of the liquid keeps this cool toy see-sawing back and forth for hours.

This is how the investment markets work. When too many people buy into a market, a category or a class, that area fills up. The law of supply and demand kicks in and the price soars higher. When the price far outweighs the investment's earnings, equity and cash flows, the price drops. It's like gravity — the higher it rises, the harder it falls.

People's emotions and lack of understanding is what makes markets move up or down in the short term.

The quality, earnings, and profitability of a company are what make prices go up over the long term.

You'll never know when the ups and downs will

happen. Sadly, people continue to get sucked into the belief that a market, stock, or category will continue to go up and never come down.

Look at the gold and silver market ups and downs. Look at the 1999 great tech crash. It took the NASDAQ fifteen years to break its highest level. These new recovery highs have just pulled back. Now in 2016, the NASDAQ is still below its 1999 highs. This not only affects prices but people's entire being.

During the time of the tech boom, people left their jobs to become day traders. Interestingly enough, I've not run into a single person who is making a living out of day trading.

Even in those go-go years, people ignored the tides. In 1999 the P/E ratios were in the 50+ range. I remember seeing the "experts" on the investment news stations saying the normal P/E range of 15-20 didn't apply anymore as this was

> P/E Ratio is the Price to Earnings. The Average for the S&P500 is around 18. This means that it takes 18 years for the earnings of a company to repay you for what you've spent per share

a new ERA. Anytime I hear this, I know I'm listening to a new line of *you-know-what*.

Then again in 2003-2006, people were buying land and real estate like crazy. Yet again I listened to the "experts" saying the new P/R ratio didn't matter anymore.

This was a new ERA. There we go again with the same line. I think we all know what happened to people who bought property during this period of time.

There are THREE types of strategies to investing and there are THREE ways to invest.

The three types of strategies to investing are:

1) Market timing.
2) Investment selection.
3) Asset allocation.

In a study known as the Brinson-Beebower study, (Determinants of Portfolio Performance, published in the Financial Analysts Journal, 1986) the researchers took ninety of the country's largest pension managers and looked back at twenty years of history. They found the returns attributed to these large institutional managers were due to the following:

> **Market timing accounted for less than 2% of the returns.**
> **Investment selection, trying to pick the next winner, accounted for less than 4% of the returns.**
> **Asset allocation accounted for more than 94% of their returns.**

I don't know about you, but I like the high percentage of wins using asset allocation. Sometimes, we have to learn

70

from those who have already been there.

If you were trying to cross a minefield, what would be the best way? DON'T BE FIRST. Once someone else has crossed a minefield, simply follow in their footsteps.

Follow those who have already succeeded, not just those who want to

> P/R is Price to Rent Ratio. It is the price of the house divided by the annual rents. The average is between 12-16.

instruct you. In later chapters, I will help you find and rate a financial advisor. If that financial advisor has not done it themselves and been successful then why should you follow them?

Now let's explore each type of investment strategy and ask yourself: which of these am I using?

MARKET TIMING

What I find interesting is so many people use market timing but will never admit it. They're what I call "closet timers."

Recently, I had a retiree in my office who managed to increase his portfolio in the recent market boom from 1.8 million to 2.4 million. With the recent downturn it went back to 1.8 million. His portfolio went down by $600,000 in four months.

If he were twenty-five years old, I would say his

portfolio design was fine and he should hold.

The portfolio he designed for himself was a high income portfolio in which the dividend rate was about 8%. However, the portfolio was very volatile with a standard deviation (Volatility Risk) of almost 31%.

He felt he was perfectly competent in designing his own portfolio because he had a degree in economics from 42 years ago.

He also felt very confident because he bought all the investment newsletters and went along with their judgment.

This was a mistake because he needed $100,000 a year from his portfolio. This equated to approximately a 5.5% distribution.

I tried explaining to him that while I did not disagree with the portfolio design, it was better suited for someone in their twenties, not in their mid-70s with a required minimum distribution and an income distribution rate of 5.5%.

> The old rule was that a 4% distribution was safe, but after the recent market volatility, most experts have reduced that to 2% to 2.5% as a safe distribution rate

He argued and argued that the markets would come back. I further explained that a dividend portfolio works when, and only when, you're able to reinvest the dividends to take advantage of the down times.

72

I also explained a 25% bond and 75% stock allocation has actually outperformed a 100% stock position in most rolling or trailing back tests.

I explained if he only needed 2% from the portfolio, the portfolio would be fine. If he needs 5.5% of the portfolio, he would have to take out a majority of the dividends. This does not allow him to reinvest when the markets are down. In a dividend portfolio this is the way the portfolio grows and is how risk is reduced.

I also questioned him on his strategy, his buys and sells, and his timing. He explained he would wait until an investment bottomed out and then he would buy it. I asked him how he knows when it's at the bottom. Being the Econ graduate he was, he said, "I just know."

I asked him if he followed this rule then, why was his account value back to the original value that it was four years ago? Shouldn't he have sold when it was at 2.4 million? No answer!

To make a long story short, his belief system got in his way and he couldn't see why this was a mistake. His was a combination of investment arrogance, fear, and control.

His wife had sat in on every meeting and understood. She wanted to move to a more Sustainable Portfolio model with less risk.

What's interesting is she had no degree and hadn't read a single newsletter, but she intuitively understood the right way to structure it.

Why market timing does not work consistently.

- ➤ You cannot tell which investments will perform better over any period of time.
- ➤ A short-term win is like winning at gambling. It gives you a false sense of confidence.
- ➤ You never know when the high or the low really is.

While you cannot time the market, you can determine if you're overpaying for an investment based on fundamental analysis, cash flows, etc. This is why dollar cost averaging in and dollar cost averaging out (referred to as systematic withdrawals), is a risk reduction strategy for retirement.

Investment Selection.

This is where you do deep research, buy newsletters or just have a "feeling" about a single investment. You buy this investment because you think it will be the "big winner."

Why investment selection <u>on its own</u> does not work.

For every Google or Apple there are 3,000 other investments that fail. Ray Dalio (Manager of the largest hedge fund) and Warren Buffet, with all their millions of investment research, still make huge mistakes, but they can

74

afford it.

While it's next to impossible to invest in the next BIG WINNER, it's possible to understand what quality is.

I would suggest reading the book *Buffettology* (Mary Buffet and David Clark). It's written by Mary Buffet, who explains how to understand Warren's fundamental analysis to investing in stocks. On a short note, Warren's normal hold strategy is no less than ten years!

I would also suggest reading *The Intelligent Investor, Revised Edition* (Benjamin Graham) (Audiobook format – read by Luke Daniels), *Uncommon Stocks – Uncommon Profits* (Phillip Fisher), *Security Analysis* (Benjamin Graham) and *One Up on Wall Street* (Peter Lynch).

Learning how to analyze the fundamentals and the right buy-in methods is a discussion for an entirely different book. Let's focus on the most successful strategy — asset allocation.

Do you believe that no one can guess or pick the best asset classes or categories in the investment markets? If you believe this, asset allocation is the best way to structure your money. In order to create an asset allocation plan, you have to know what the areas to invest into each allocation are.

There are twenty-seven asset sub-classes falling under four major asset classes.

The four major asset classes are:

> **Stocks**
> **Bonds**
> **Real Estate**
> **Alternative**

Under each major asset class are sub-classes. The stock sub-classes are:

> **Small Cap Domestic**
> **Small Cap International Developed**
> **Small Cap International Emerging**
> **Large Cap Domestic**
> **Large Cap International Developed**
> **Large Cap International Emerging**
> **Preferred Stocks**

You might be wondering why I don't list mid-cap stocks. This is because, in my opinion, there's so little difference in volatility and performance between small cap and mid-cap, I have grouped them into small cap.

There are also many different opinions of what separates a small cap from a mid-cap stock. Is it the ten billion mark of capitalization or is it the five billion mark? Depending on the institution, the manager or the research source, this opinion can vary.

Under the bond sub-class, you have:

> - **Short Term Government**
> - **Intermediate Term Government**
> - **Long Term Government**
> - **International Government**
> - **Convertibles**
> - **Short Term Corporate**
> - **Intermediate Term Corporate**
> - **Long Term Corporate**
> - **High Yield**

Within each group you also have ratings from high quality to low quality. I also put fixed or equity indexed annuities into the bond category as they best represent this class of investment. These types of annuities have low to no volatility, ordinary income tax, a maturity date, and a rating. I purposely did not state that Municipals are in the bond category. They are in the bond category but you can swap for the government bonds depending on the rating, maturity, and your tax bracket.

Under Real Estate you have:
> - **Personally owned real estate**
> - **Tenants in common**
> - **Public listed REITs**
> - **Non-listed REITs.**

Under the alternative asset class are:
- **Commodities**
- **Peer to peer investing or lending**
- **Private equity**
- **Hard money lending**
- **Business lending**
- **Business development companies.**

The key to getting asset allocation to work for you is to structure your investment model to integrate with your cash flow and income.

(WARNING - DO NOT ARBITRARILY PICK AN ASSET ALLOCATION MODEL - THIS SHOULD ONLY BE DONE AFTER YOUR RETIREMENT PLAN AND CALCULATIONS ARE COMPLETED.)

Many investors pick their asset allocation models like they order food at a restaurant.

A menu has the prices on the right. When some people are out to dinner, they scan the right side of the menu until they find something in their price range. It's usually liver and onions. I apologize if you like liver and onions but other than the price, I just don't get it.

When some people choose their investments, they scan the right side of the investment selection form or brochure.

This is where the most recent returns are shown. These

same people chose their investments based on the most recent highest returns. This is a big mistake.

Instead of choosing your model based upon the most recent returns, you're first going to understand which model will fit your TOTAL RETIREMENT FREEDOM PLAN.

This is based on your expenses, your time period, your cash flows, your tax bracket, the amount of insurance you currently have, and your current health. Once you've done this, then, and only then, can you choose the asset allocation model.

These asset allocation models might be titled as very conservative, conservative, moderate and aggressive. For example, a very conservative model may be comprised of:

➤ **80% Bonds**
➤ **10% Stock**
➤ **5% Real Estate**
➤ **5% Alternatives**

Whereas an aggressive model may be:

➤ **50% Stock**
➤ **20% Real Estate**
➤ **20% Alternatives**
➤ **10% Bonds**

Each of these models will have a volatility risk which can be estimated based on its mixture. If you remember from the prior chapter, this is referred to as the standard deviation.

Once volatility risk has been compared to your TOTAL RETIREMENT FREEDOM PLAN, you can determine if it's acceptable.

Acceptable for what you can emotionally handle, but also for what your plan sustainability can handle.

Your second step is to create an ongoing process and system of how to know when to make changes. This means setting a rules-based system on when to rebalance.

Calendar rebalance means that you set a frequency to rebalance. Don't rebalance any more frequently than quarterly if you use calendar-based rebalance.

Tolerance band rebalance means you set a rule that says if your asset classes or underlying categories get out of balance by a certain percentage, it triggers a rebalance.

If you use tolerance rebalance, do not rebalance by any less than 15%.

Don't change your asset allocation rules! If markets suddenly drop or increase, stick by your rules.

Only change your model based on YOUR changes in health, goals, or financial conditions. **Let me this state again, do not change your model based on short-term market fluctuations.**

CONFUSING ASSET ALLOCATION WITH DIVERSIFICATION

You can imagine what I've seen in portfolio designs over the years.

In many of these cases, the client believed they had an asset allocation plan or model. In fact, most of the time all they really had was a diversification plan.

In most plans there's still too much risk because they're over-allocated to one or more categories or classes.

This is also called overlap. Imagine you invest in one hundred stocks, but they're all in small cap domestics and large cap domestics.

Do you have an asset allocation model or only a diversified model? This diversified, non-allocated portfolio will still follow the ups and down of the US stock market. When our domestic stock market goes up, this portfolio goes up. When our domestic markets go down, so does this portfolio.

If the stocks went into a period of decline while bonds were going up, this stock portfolio would lose out due to being concentrated in what might have been thought to be the next winning category.

In short, you can have one hundred stocks in different companies which would give you diversification, but not asset allocation.

Over the long term, a portfolio mix of both stock,

bonds, real estate, and alternatives have shown to have the highest performance and the lowest volatility.

The key is mixing them correctly to match your personal financial fingerprint to your model. This is true asset allocation.

Here's a common question: Can you have an asset allocation model and still be diversified? The answer is yes.

The proper way is to create your asset allocation model based on your cash flows. This determines the percentages you allocate to each asset class and subsequently to each asset sub-class.

If you allocate a certain percentage to each category, then you should diversify within that category.

As an example, if your plan creates a 20% allocation in large cap domestic stocks, diversify to different investments within that asset category.

If you use three or four Exchange Traded Funds (ETFs) that use large cap stocks, you may end up with between four hundred and one thousand stocks.

When you're using ETFs, you need to make sure you're not simply overlapping the same stocks within each ETF. There are tools available to run overlap reports to prevent this from happening. I'll cover those tools in the resource and tool section of this book. If you have enough in your portfolio you can use individual stocks.

I would not suggest investing in individual stocks with less than $100,000. The cost of buys and sells and lack of diversification would make ETFs a better choice.

The discussion of making mistakes on how to invest would be missing a major component if I left out the options of the channels to investing. There are different channels depending on the type of investment and the amount you have to invest.

The first and most common channel is the stocks and bond channel. Within stocks and bonds, there are three ways to invest:

- ➤ Individual Issue
- ➤ Mutual Fund
- ➤ ETFs (Exchange Traded Funds)

Within the real estate channel there are four ways to invest:

- ➤ Individual Ownership
- ➤ Private or Non-Listed REIT or Partnership
- ➤ Public REIT or ETF
- ➤ Peer-to-Peer

Lastly, within the insurance and annuity world, there are eight ways to invest:

- ➤ Variable Annuities
- ➤ Fixed Index Annuities
- ➤ Traditional Fixed Annuity

- ➤ Immediate Annuities
- ➤ Indexed Universal Life
- ➤ Variable Life
- ➤ Whole Life
- ➤ Universal Life

We'll start with a very basic understanding of each channel.

Stocks and Bonds

I don't have an opinion that ETFs are better or worse than buying individual issues. Comparing ETF models versus individual stock models within Morningstar, we know that individual issue stock models have almost doubled the returns of ETF models. The difference is the volatility on the stock models also doubles.

A good rule of thumb is to use ETFs in accounts in which there is either too little to get proper diversification with individual issues, or there's a need to keep the volatility lower but still have equity allocations.

I like ETFs as a core holding because they invest under the philosophy called Passive Investing.

Passive Investing is what John Bogle, founder of Vanguard invented more than four decades ago. It's now known by the name of Indexing.

Indexing is a simple yet proven way to invest money into a portfolio. This all assumes you don't believe a person

84

can time the market or guess the next big winner.

On the other side of the investment philosophy you have active management.

Active management depends on a manager buying and selling the investments for you. Active management presumes you believe someone can time the market or can pick the next Google or Amazon.

You can, however, get a concentrated managed portfolio of individual stocks that are handpicked and the manager has very little turnover. I turn back to the example of Morningstar Managed Portfolios.

Their individual selected contrarian stock portfolios have less than a 5% turnover but have doubled the performance of their ETF models in the last five years up to the date of June 1, 2016. They have essentially created a passive strategy with a concentrated set of stocks. The difference between passive and active management is the turnover ratio.

I have a deep philosophical disagreement with the belief that managers can out-buy or sell the market; therefore, I'm adamantly opposed to variable annuities, variable life, and open-ended mutual funds.

There are mechanical and design flaws within these types of investments that benefit the issuers. Variable annuities and variable life both use mutual funds and therefore share these fundamental design flaws. There's also up to a fivefold increase in fees by using open-ended mutual funds, variable annuities or variable life as compared to ETFs or individual stocks.

These design flaws are why I would suggest staying as far away from mutual funds (open-ended) as possible. Here are more reasons to stay away from them:

- Excessive fees.
- No way to control the actual investment allocation (referred to as investment sway). The mutual fund manager is only required to invest 65% of your money in the fund prospectus objective.
- Too many back door deals that cost you money. Most mutual funds have some type of selling agreement with a brokerage firm. This increases your fees due to commissions paid to advisors, costs to buy and sell the securities within the fund, and marketing costs.
- Uncontrollable tax effects. Due to tax rules, the mutual fund must distribute taxable income to you even though the fund might be down in price.
- No control. Investing in a mutual fund is like riding the city bus. You have to go where the bus driver — or in this case the fund manager — takes you, even if it's opposite of the market. In many cases, managers time it wrong and take money out of the market while it's going up. They have also bought in at the high because

they have to. In a sense, a mutual fund manager is handcuffed because of how a mutual fund is structured. Fund managers underperform the indexed strategies 84% of the time. Why bet on the 16% chance of winning?

In an extension of a prior study, Laurent Barras, O. Scaillet and Russ Wermer expanded on a study that updated these numbers to show that mutual fund managers have only outperformed the markets 1% of the time. There are a lot of reasons they cite, all of which I agree with.

As a side note, while I don't agree with variable annuities, there are two low-cost carriers that might work if you have to have one. These carriers are Fidelity and Vanguard. While a remote strategy, if you want the upside of the market and life insurance without having to pass a physical, these variable annuities might work as long as you use the index choices within the annuity wrapper.

I'm sure you know what is coming next: our legal department wants to make sure I tell you not to invest in these without the prior help or analysis from a fiduciary advisor.

.

Real Estate

In my experience, there are only four ways of investing in real estate: directly, non-listed REITs, public listed REITs or ETFs, and Peer-to-Peer.

One of the main reasons I don't like private REITs or partnerships is lack of transparency. Here's the complete list of problems that I've seen with private REITs.

> ➢ Partners can increase their salaries with no vote from investors if a limited partnership, or other entity, allows them this flexibility.
> ➢ It's hard to find out if the organizers have any criminal or bankruptcy background. We do the due diligence for clients who are presented with these types of real estate deals. In the last four proposals our clients received to invest, we sent out our due diligence questionnaire. This asks for information on the partners, the partnership agreement, and details on the actual project. Not only did these salespeople not send us any of the information, they've not contacted any of our clients again.
> ➢ Tax issues. If you've ever had to deal with partnerships, you know what a tax nightmare it can be. Partnerships produce passive income losses which can only be used against passive income gains. Be very careful of the promises of tax write-offs. While you

might get the paper loss, you may never be able to actually write off the deductions.

- ➤ Valuation issues. Partnerships and private issue REITs are types of investments which are next to impossible to determine the value of a share or interest. If you have a retirement plan, this causes even more issues. For many years, these investments would issue with a par value of $10.00 or $25.00 per share. For years, clients would get statements telling them they had a certain amount in value. Recently, the SEC required these REITs, or partnerships, to use a different pricing method. Clients' share values dropped substantially compared to their prior valuations, shocking investors. It's even more of a nightmare if you have required minimum distributions due and you have no liquidity in the investment.

Individual real estate comes with its own risks and responsibilities which must be considered. Individual real estate investing may have the best tax outcome and potential for you but it comes with the most risk.

Take it from someone who used to own over thirty-eight units and managed over thirty units of other investors' real estate. When that pipe bursts at 2:00am, or the kitchen fire happens at 4:00am, you're the one who has to deal with it.

Owning rental properties is owning a small business

and must be thought of as such, as opposed to looking at it purely as a passive investment.

You also take on personal liability, so unless you've structured your business the correct way, you may lose more than your original investment.

One of my mentors taught me risk is defined as how much you could lose.

In a stock investment, the maximum you can lose is your original investment. If that company gets sued and goes out of business, they cannot transfer that liability to you, personally.

If you own a rental property and someone sues you, you can lose every dime you've ever earned and saved. If you would like to learn more about this, you can go to our video education on this by going to

www.kenhimmler.com/trf/assetprotection

Investing in equity or loans tied to real estate through peer-to-peer investing is a newer way to invest.

It's shown to be a very good diversified alternative to the more common ways to invest in real estate.

It takes advantage of web technology to diversify between many different projects, loans, and partial equity positions.

It allows you to diversify between commercial, office, residential, and even land acquisition in small partitions.

I'm in favor of this because it allows you to diversify to different regions of the country to reduce your risk.

I also like this method because the companies that offer this have a process in place. Their process is the same type that a billion-dollar institutional real estate company would use to find and research property before investing. They offer the background on the developer, the credit rating, and the past projects. They also offer the ability to see what the current project returns are, based on appraisals and generally acceptable real estate valuation methodologies.

If you wanted to really learn how to value a property and determine its viability, you can learn a lot from their processes.

You can also go to our web site as we have more information on peer-to-peer real estate investing.

www.kenhimmler.com/trf/p2p

Public REITS are also a great way to obtain diversification with better liquidity than the individual or peer-to-peer investments. The other advantages of using an ETF, REIT, or a closed-end fund is that you can insure the loss.

Public listed REITs are eligible for PUT buying. PUTs can be used to insure the loss of principal, which cannot be done with individually owned, non-listed, or peer-to-peer owned real estate investments.

Listed REITs are also simple to put into IRAs and other types of accounts. When you invest in an individual property or a non-public partnership, the rules and laws in a retirement plan get very complex and dangerous.

I also like the public REITs better because they're marked to the market, which means that you know what they are really worth on a day-to-day basis; plus, they're liquid.

Lastly, a publicly traded REIT also allows very easy tax planning due to the ability to swap and harvest between accounts. This is not possible with an individually owned property, non-public REIT, or a peer-to-peer investment.

Annuities

If you've learned anything about me, you already know I have two types of investments I don't like. The first is open-ended mutual funds and the second is either variable annuities or variable life insurance.

If a person needs life insurance but is uninsurable, it might be a reason why I might recommend a variable annuity. These cases are so remote that I've only seen it a few times in thirty-plus years.

As I mentioned before, I would only recommend two companies, Fidelity and Vanguard. These are the only two companies that sell a variable annuity with reasonable expenses, allowable riders, and death benefits for a low and reasonable cost.

We make every effort to keep our lists updated so you may want to join our newsletter to keep in the "Know." You can access by going to:

www.kenhimmler.com/ifn

Other than the brokerage world, I'm not the only person who disagrees with these variable products. If you want other opinions, Google the following:

➤ Suze Orman Video on Variable Life
➤ Suze Orman on Variable Annuities
➤ Forbes on Variable Annuities

If variable annuities are too high in expenses and risk, then what other types of annuities can you invest in?

Fixed annuities are certainly appropriate when interest rates are higher. When rates are low, fixed annuities are better than bank CDs but not by much.

There's another type of annuity which has only been around since the mid-1990s. These types of annuities are referred to as EIAs, FIAs, or, in long form, Equity Indexed Annuities.

A Fixed Indexed Annuity is quite simple. Take away all the confusion insurance agents might add and you end up with a bond replacement.

An immediate annuity is most likely the cause of most people's misunderstanding, apprehension or confusion about annuities.

When you see bad press about annuities it's usually about these types of annuities. An immediate annuity is when you give a lump sum to the insurance company with a promise they'll pay a stream of income over an agreed-upon period of time.

Once the agreed-upon time has expired, there's no more money.

Many people don't like this idea because of the risk. Imagine you buy a life-only annuity on Monday and die on Tuesday. All the money is gone and does not pass onto your family.

Another negative with an immediate annuity is, while they promise a large income, when interest rates are low they lock in rates at a very low level.

A positive is if this type of annuity is done outside of a retirement plan, it can be structured to be tax efficient. One reason for this tax efficiency is when you get your payment, you are also getting part of your principal back, tax free.

You're better off only using an immediate annuity as a bond replacement strategy when rates are very high. The only other alternative is to set the payout period for a short period, such as five years.

You use this strategy when you're waiting out a market crash or selling a business or a home, etc. Like any idea or strategy, there are also exceptions.

There are specialized immediate annuities called medically underwritten annuities. I'm not opposed to this in the right situation. A medically underwritten annuity is when you have a life-shortening health condition.

Normal annuity or mortality tables get shortened due to your health.

If you're age 65 and you have a serious health condition, after a medical exam, (paid for by the insurance company) you might be able to invest into a medically underwritten annuity and the insurance company uses an age of 75, or ten years older than you really are.

This would give you a much higher payout than a normal immediate annuity based on your true age.

In planning, this might work to leverage other areas of your plan.
Again, it's not that these are bad or good, they're a tool to be used in the right situation. When you structure these investments, it's also important for you to make sure you're not making a tax mistake.

LACK OF STRATEGIC TAX PLANNING

By now you've learned there are certain things you can and cannot control. You've also started to refocus your energy on things you can control.

An area you can control is your tax plan. I think every

American complains about the tax system but few do anything about it.

Every minute complaining about our tax system is a minute you could be reworking your personal tax plan to pay less.

You're an American with all the rights and abilities to structure your tax plan for the lowest legal tax possible. In no way am I encouraging you to lie on your tax returns. The good news: you don't need to. There are plenty of tax strategies to reduce or, in some cases, eliminate your income taxes. You just need to learn for yourself how to do it or hire someone who knows how.

> "The difference between death and taxes is death doesn't get worse very time Congress meets."
>
> **Will Rogers**

Will your accountant or CPA do this for you? I don't know. But I can tell you that we find ways to structure clients' taxes to save them money in about nine out of ten cases. Those same people we save taxes for have CPAs, accountants, or have tried their hand at it by using Turbo Tax (or some other tax program) but are still overpaying their taxes.

Two recent experiences with people trying to do it themselves show that unless you know how to do this, it can cost you much more than having someone do it for you who knows what they are doing.

A new client came in who is a very smart person. He's in the legal community, and has run his own investments and taxes for years. He wanted someone to review what he was doing.

Without getting into all the details, I picked up a mistake in the first five minutes on his tax returns related to his rental properties.

He took a $108,000 rental property loss. This is not permissible as it's limited to $25,000. I've seen this before. People will click a little box on the tax program that asks if they are a professional real estate person. This means they spend more than 750 hours a year and it's their primary business.

Being this person was a lawyer first and a real estate investor second, he didn't meet this test. Therefore, by clicking on this one little box, it allowed a deduction of $83,000 more than he was entitled to. If he gets audited, he will incur a large penalty and interest, plus the tax.

> "I am proud to be paying taxes in the United States. The only thing is could be just as proud for half of the money." **Arthur Godfrey**

In the second case, an engineer who retired from MIT was doing her own tax returns. In the tax program, she entered the value of the property as she understood the instructions. The problem? She entered the value of the property and the land value together.

This caused her to depreciate the entire value which, again, is not allowed. She had done this for years, which could cause hundreds of thousands of dollars in back taxes, penalties, and interest.

If you do hire someone, it doesn't mean you hired the right person. The person you hire may not know or understand tax planning and may simply be a tax preparer.

The CPA exam has a very small part on personal tax planning. There's more devoted to corporate and auditing on the CPA exam than on personal tax planning.

Even if you have a CPA who really understands tax planning, it still may not be their business model to give you tax planning advice. The CPA's practice may be structured for tax preparation and not tax planning.

To have a tax planning department within a tax practice means the CPA has to spend considerable dollars on tax planning software and tools. It means that they will have to build out complex models and 'what if' scenarios to create the tax plans for you. This type of planning takes tools, time, expertise, and expense.

> "For a nation to try to tax itself into prosperity is like a man standing in bucket and trying to life himself up by the handle." **Winston Churchill**

If you're going to a simple tax preparation service, you may not even be getting some of the basics in tax reduction planning.

Recently, a new client hired me for their tax planning. Upon review, I found for years they'd owned a second property in the Georgetown area of Washington, D.C. They'd been letting their daughter stay there and she'd been paying all the bills such as the Homeowner's Association dues. Their tax preparer never told them this property was eligible as a rental property with all the deductions available. This mistake has cost them tens of thousands of dollars in lost deductions.

This brings me to the last reason why you may not be getting tax planning advice. In the early 1990s, I left my first firm I worked for. I was preparing over 150 tax returns, both personal and corporate every year.

When it got down to crunch time, I didn't have time to take Mr. and Mrs. Jones tax return out and spend hours creating 'what if' scenarios. It was time to get those returns prepared and out the door. In some cases, I identified and proposed tax saving ideas to certain clients. I explained it may take an extra hour or two of billable time to calculate the potential. In most of

> "The hardest thing in the world to understand is the income tax." **Albert Einstein**

these cases the client didn't want to pay for the time to get tax planning done.

There's a large gap between tax preparation and tax

planning. Which one are you getting now? If you're not paying a separate fee for tax planning, rest assured, you're only getting tax preparation. This means you may be paying thousands if not millions of dollars in too much tax.

Here are some of the basic tax mistakes I find people make:

➤ Having taxable dividends and/or interest show up on the 1040.
➤ Not using QLACs and other tax reduction strategies to reduce the tax on RMDs.
➤ Not computing ROTH conversions every year.
➤ Trying to deduct medical insurance and expenses on Schedule A and taking the 10% of AGI reduction.
➤ Earning too much on 1040 and wiping out itemized deductions, such as mortgage interest, property taxes, and medical.
➤ Not structuring RMDs from IRAs correctly and having too much income, creating trigger taxes.
➤ Not structuring RMDs correctly and causing the Medicare income-based penalty.
➤ Earning too much income on the 1040 and losing rental property deductions.
➤ Paying taxes on life insurance dividends.
➤ Not taking losses on surrendered life insurance and annuities.

- Not getting tax deductions on life insurance premiums.
- Having passive losses and not deducting them.
- Having the wrong investments placed in the wrong accounts. As an example, having capital gain property invested in retirement plans which increases and possibly doubles the taxation on the investment.
- Not sheltering taxable interest when it's not being used.
- Not having a plan to take distributions for retirement in the most tax efficient way possible.
- Naming the wrong beneficiary sequence on retirement plans or annuities.
- Naming the wrong owners of an annuity, such as naming a trust as an owner.
- Not understanding the RMD rules and paying penalties.
- Not utilizing GAMMA.

In the fiduciary advisor community, we're all talking about the recent study done by Morningstar on GAMMA. This study brings to light the fact that applying strategies and techniques above

> GAMMA is the term for efficiency of investment management through lowering of fees, correct tax allocation, tax harvesting and distribution strategy.

just investment selection can increase your income by up to 29%. Interestingly enough, at no time did they study any effect other than the increase in net returns due to investment structure. Now imagine you went beyond that and added tax structure to all the other parts of your financial life. What amount of increase above the 29% would you now see?

I could fill an entire book with tax strategies but I'm sure you can see tax planning is very different than tax preparation.

DISTRIBUTION STRATEGY VS. ACCUMULATION STRATEGY

One of the mistakes that causes people not to achieve their full retirement or financial potential is not recognizing the difference between the accumulation stage and the distribution stage.

A reason for this knowledge gap is most of the financial institutions are structured for accumulation, not distribution.

If the financial institutions are not structured for distribution then they don't need to teach it to their salespeople, their advisors, or their clients.

Most advisors which learn distribution techniques do this on their own through certification courses or other higher education.

Think about it this way, if the financial institution gets paid for accumulating assets, why would they want to teach their advisors or clients how to take more out?

> When you move from the Accumulation Stage to the Distribution Stage you must change the tax, investment and entire structure of your plan.

There's another reason you'll not find a lot of experts in the distribution planning arena.

The knowledge base needed for accumulation planning is much less than the expertise needed for distribution planning. When you're focused on accumulation, you want to know these areas:

- ➤ What are the limits of saving money into certain type of retirement plans?
- ➤ What are the optimal investments to grow your money?
- ➤ What are the risks and fees on different investments?

While you are in the accumulation stage, you can get over mistakes easier because you have income from working.

Once you retire and your income is dependent on your assets, you have less tolerance for mistakes.

When you're working with an advisor who specializes in distribution planning they need to be at a much higher knowledge level.

If you're going to do your own retirement planning, you'll also need to know the following:

> ➢ How to run future value calculations on cash flows and the best places from which to take funds for cash flow.
> ➢ What method and age should you file for Social Security?
> ➢ What are the ownership and naming rules on IRAs and Annuities?
> ➢ How to structure trusts and wills.
> ➢ How to structure cash flows for minimum income taxation. Which of the six distribution methods do you use? Do you use a static method or a combination method?
> ➢ How to run stress tests on health care, inflation, premature death, changes in income taxation, and investment risks to assure supporting your cash flow for the future.
> ➢ How to run calculations to determine if you should use your house for annuity income.

> ➢ How to determine which assets to turn on or off for income each year.
> ➢ How to make charitable deductions in the most tax efficient way possible.
> ➢ How to create LLCs or corporations to provide asset

protection on personal homes or investment properties.

➤ What to do to provide the lowest cost protection against long-term care.

➤ What to do to provide protection against lost Social Security or pensions in case of death.

➤ How to assure the children's and/or grandchildren's money is protected.

➤ How to make sure that healthcare documents, such as durable power of attorneys and healthcare powers, are all tied in correctly to the rest of the assets.

➤ How to make sure all assets are titled correctly into the trusts to make sure the trust works. This includes the new rules on passwords and digital asset rights.

➤ How to structure an asset allocation model that fits the cash flow distribution needs.

➤ How to structure an asset allocation model to reduce volatility risk.

➤ How to structure an asset allocation model with the lowest possible fees.

With this long list of skills needed for distribution planning I would suggest it is much easier to accumulate funds than it is to distribute them correctly and efficiently.

STEPS FOR ACCUMULATION

Step 1- Determine the number of years until distributions begin.

Step 2- Allocate the following into ETFs (Stocks, if you have enough in your investments) by buying the funds every quarter in the amount you can afford to invest. Do not worry about the ups or downs.

For a 10 Year Plan:
> ✓ 60% Stock; 40% Bonds

For a 20 Year Plan:
> ✓ 80 Stock; 20% Bonds

For more than 30 years:
> ✓ 90% Stock; 10% Bonds

Step 3 - Five years before you plan on making distributions, create a distribution plan that will systematically reduce the amount of volatility risk.

You should have a distribution plan done at least five years prior to retirement so you can calculate the amount of equity/bond/real estate appropriate once you do retire. Don't plan on making those types of sweeping changes on your asset allocation right before retirement.

You cannot control market fluctuations; therefore, you cannot protect against a reduction in markets at a certain time.

As I said before, the accumulation phase is actually quite simple. There are still fundamental decisions such as:

- ➤ Do I buy a house or rent?
- ➤ Do I lease, buy, or loan my automobile?
- ➤ Do I buy term insurance or cash value life insurance?
- ➤ What deductible and coverages do I take on auto, home, and health?
- ➤ How much do I save?
- ➤ Do I put money away before tax or use a ROTH?

These are all very simple calculations. While you're working, mistakes can be overlooked as you have income to make up for blunders. When you're retired every dollar counts — you cannot afford financial missteps.

In either case, I am assuming you are reading on because you're either in the distribution phase of your life or you're coming up on it quick. In the next section we'll discuss what obstacles are ahead of you.

LACK OF A PROTECTION STRATEGY

One of my great idols is Warren Buffett. I like his basic and grounded approach to investments. He has a philosophy each of his employees abide by. He calls this the "two rules to investing." Rule 1 is, don't lose money. Rule 2 is, see Rule 1.

While main street media and Hollywood create a belief that investment titans have risked everything to get ahead, real life is actually quite different.

Ray Dalio, Warren Buffet, John Bogle, Sir John Templeton and other masters of the investment universe use a very different approach.

Their approach is a measurement of risk vs. reward. What I've found so interesting is that these investment wizards don't risk very much. They look for investments with a high return but a low risk. They also employ protection strategies.

A protection strategy may be done by hedging or insuring. Whichever way is chosen, it's interesting to see the richest investors insuring their risks while the smallest investors lay all the chips on a single roll of the dice.

It's also stunning to me when the average person will not think twice about insuring their home against fire or damage or insuring their $30,000 automobile against dents or dings. On the other hand, they'll leave their multi-million-dollar portfolio totally at risk uninsured and not understanding their risk.

Whether you decide to insure or protect your portfolio through hedges, offsets, puts, or annuities, the real question is what have you done to protect your money?

If you're driving, you hopefully look at the speed signs and then look at your speedometer to know if you're staying in the safe zone.

Are you doing the same thing with your money? Have you figured out how much risk you can really afford in order to meet your goals? Are you fully aware of the risk you're taking on your portfolio?

If you converted your portfolio to a number between 1 and 100 (100 being the highest risk), do you know where you are?

Protection is not limited to your investments, auto, or home. You're also at risk of loss of income, loss of life, healthcare expense, lawsuit, or even probate or surrogate expenses.

We'll start with loss of income as most people either understand or already have insurance covering their home or auto.

There are generally two stages in everyone's life. The People at Work Stage and then the Money at Work Stage.

While you're still in the People at Work Stage, you're at risk if you lose your job or income due to a disability. You may never get to accumulate enough to get to the Money at Work Stage, if your income producing ability gets cut short.

To protect against a disability risk you should make

sure you have disability insurance. Your disability insurance should be calculated to cover the need and risk based on your TOTAL RETIREMENT FREEDOM PLAN. You should also make sure it's structured correctly to obtain the tax benefits allowed.

We recently advised a client of ours, a fifty-year-old realtor making a million dollars a year, to buy disability insurance. The annual cost was $10,000 to cover $250,000 a year in case she couldn't work.

She was advised by her CPA, not us, to pay the premiums out of pocket and not through the business. The CPA's rationale was if she needed the benefit, the benefit would be tax free.

We disagreed and advised her to pay the premiums out of her business. Our reason was she would be able to take a 4,000 deduction on the premiums due to her being in a 40% tax bracket.

Our strategy brought her net cost down to only $6,000 per year. I explained if she did become disabled, her income would much be less. The smaller income would result in the tax bracket being one third of her current bracket.

I would much rather have someone get the present value of the reduced cost and tax deduction now, especially if she never becomes disabled.

By her taking the deduction she has at least saved $4,000 a year.

The need for disability to protect your earning ability

110

is very important, don't overlook this if you're still working.

Life insurance. Life insurance has traditionally been a way to cover a spouse or children in case of premature death.

It's also been used as a way to pay off debts. Most people never think about life insurance as a way to pay off tax debt on IRAs or annuities at death. Tax at death is just as much a debt as a mortgage.

Life insurance is simply a leveraging device. It allows you to obtain millions of dollars of leverage with only pennies on the dollar in cost.

If you have to pay your light bill for $1,000, imagine giving $100.00 to the insurance company and they pay the $1,000 bill for you.

This example is how life insurance should be viewed, as a discounted way to pay an eventual bill.

If you're still working and there's someone else dependent on your People at Work energy, then life insurance is important because you're insuring the loss of your income in case of your premature death.

Long-term care expenses. Thirty years ago, when I first started calculating client's futures, there was a one in ten chance someone would live out their golden years in a nursing facility.

With the invention of the computer chip, our medical technology has advanced more in the last thirty years than in the last 10,000 years of mankind.

With advances like these, we've seen longer life spans. Even though we're living longer we're not guaranteed health.

Statistics show that 7 out of 10 people will live out their lives in either a nursing facility or needing in-home nursing care. This means more expense at an average national cost of $77,000 per year.

This added expense could devastate a family's financial security. The costs really depend on where you live and the level of care and facility.

In some cases, it's worse when someone needs long term care vs. dying. When we die, our expenses stop. When we get sick but need additional care we add that expense onto whatever our current expenses are.

If you're married, then you also take on the legal medical liability of your spouse. If you need nursing care, all of the family's income and assets may be needed to take care of you. This expense may leave your spouse without enough income to survive.

For certain clients, after the calculations are complete, I discover they don't need the long term care insurance.

For others, I find that without long-term care insurance, they'll be destroyed if there's a healthcare catastrophe.

There are many different ways to cover this risky expense. Annuities with long-term care riders can be an options for some. Even life insurance with a long-term care rider is now an option.

The key is to do the calculations to first see if you need it and if so, determine the best strategy.

Lawsuit protection. Depending on where you live, you may already have great asset protection. States such as Florida, Nevada, Alaska, Wyoming, and South Dakota are asset protection havens.

You must be very careful to follow the state's rules for protecting assets. Just because a state has a rule on protection does not mean that you have that protection.

As an example, after the Enron folks and OJ Simpson moved to Florida to protect their assets, Florida changed certain requirements.

Another example is if you live in Nevada, there's only $500,000 of protection on your IRAs and only $532,000 protection on your home.

You should use whatever legal strategies are available to be able to protect what you have earned. You need to make sure you're following the rules and stay up to date, making changes as needed to your plan.

Here are some of the mistakes I've seen people make with asset protection:

➢ Not having rental properties in LLCs or protective entities which would protect them.
➢ Not using ERISA-based plans when their state does not protect their IRAs.

- ➢ Not having life insurance and/or annuities owned correctly to protect them.
- ➢ Having investment accounts in personal names or in family trust names.
- ➢ Putting properties into LLCs and not having the insurance companies approve the entity as insured.

Lack of probate and surrogate protection

Many times I see clients come into my firm that only have wills. This can be a large problem, at least for the families that are left behind to sort it out.

Here's an easy way to remember how it works: "If you have a will, it will create probate." Probate can take up to two years, it's public, and can cost thousands to even hundreds of thousands of dollars to settle.

A trust can solve the probate problem, but it has to be done correctly. Even if someone has a trust, I commonly see people name children as the beneficiaries of their retirement plans or annuities.

By naming a child or spouse as the beneficiary, it bypasses the trust and does not protect the assets. I also see a majority of people that have trusts don't titled assets correctly in their trusts.

Not funding your trust fully undermines the entire reason to have one.

Lastly, the medical system has changed. Do you have an old health care power of attorney and/or a durable power of attorney in which you've named someone who is out of town? Now you may run into some major issues.

In a recent case, a new client hired me to create his plan. Before we could reform his estate plan he was rushed to the hospital. In his old document, he named his daughter on the east coast as his health care power of attorney. The hospital refused to talk with her as they could not verify her identity over the phone.

It's a new world out there with Homeland Security, the Patriot Act, HIPPA, new rules against money laundering know and AML, and healthcare privacy requirements. You may think you have protection, but it's only on paper and may not work in reality.

Now you've gotten a better idea of what some of the obstacles are that you're going to face on your journey to creating your TOTAL RETIREMENT FREEDOM PLAN.

> **HIMMLER RULE #5 If you're going to build and live in a castle, dig a big moat and fill it with giant alligators.**

Please don't let all these obstacles discourage you. At least you now know what obstacles there are. Let's first lay the groundwork for creating your plan by setting goals, collecting the data, and making a decision on how to assemble and manage it.

SET YOUR GOALS

Goal setting is an odd event or task. It's only been in the last twenty years or so that modern medicine has accepted the idea of how powerful the mind is.

Recent research has shown cancer patients who visualize good health have a higher recovery rates.

Why would a chapter on goal setting in your TOTAL RETIREMENT FREEDOM PLAN be important?

Some experts say by the time you're eighteen years old you're told NO more than forty thousand times! We're all told to live in a realistic world. What is realistic? Is this based on your perception of reality?

What if Edison listened to what everyone told him on the 9,999th time the light bulb failed? It took him over 10,000 times to get it to work.

In the 1950s, if you even whispered "in the future you could talk to your car and it would

> **HIMMLER RULE #6 That which is not desired is not seen. That which is not seen is not achieved.**

produce a map to lead you to your location", they would've thought you were nuts!

The only limit on your goals is what you believe you can achieve and, more importantly, what you're willing to do or give up to achieve them! For every goal there is a price to be paid.

What amazes me is that the average American spends more time planning their annual vacation than they do planning out their financial future.

If American's spent half the amount of time planning out their financial futures as they did their vacations, can you imagine the improvements in people's lives?

To get on the right track quickly, ask yourself the first question: What's most important about money - to me"?

You can go to the bookstore and pick up hundreds of books about goals and goal setting.

Books from **Dennis Waitley, Zig Ziglar, Anthony Robbins, Darren Hardy, Steve Chandler, Matt Furey, Brian Tracey, T. Harv Elker, Ken Blanchard, David Schwartz**, and, finally, **Jack Canfield** are the best authors to teach you about goal setting.

Anything you read here is a credit to all these great authors and leaders and what they've taught in their books. Please invest in their books and

In the mid-1800s, Commissioner of the U.S. Patent Office, Charles H. Duell, stated, "Everything that can be invested has been invested."

become a master at goal setting as this will be the key to developing your WHY.

When setting goals within a system, every one of these amazing authors has a system.

Darren Hardy speaks about having SMART goals. As

a matter of fact, he says "If you don't have SMART goals you really don't have goals at all." What is a SMART goal? It is a goal that is:

- o S-Specific.
- o M-Measurable.
- o A-Attainable.
- o R-Reasonable.
- o T-Time. (You have the ability to invest the time in attainment of the goal.)

  - ✓ Do you have goals?
  - ✓ Are they written down?
  - ✓ Are they SMART goals?

> To get a goals worksheet visit
> www.kenhimmler.com/trf/goalsworksheet

Setting Your Goals

If you're single (or married, and each person handles their own finances) then:

1. Write down as many goals as you can on your worksheet. What you think is possible is limited right now by your perception of your capability,

which may not be reality. Don't limit what you put down based on what you think your present reality is.

2. Cross-check with your values — can I accomplish these goals and stay in tune with my life values? Example: if you're a parent and your value is to be around your children, a goal that would take you away from them would not work.

3. Prioritize all your goals into a list of importance and time.

If married (and managing your finances jointly), then:

1) Complete Step 1 from above. Each partner should do their own worksheet.
2) Cross-check your values.
3) Your partner cross-checks their values.
4) Create one list of goals that you jointly agree upon.
5) Prioritize the joint goals.

You want to write down goals that you can control and achieve. Let me give you another example.

If you wrote down that you want to travel around the world by working on a cruise ship, but you have three children in school, this might be an empty wish, unless the cruise ship has an on-board school. If you're sixty years old, it might not be realistic to say

> **HIMMLER RULE #7 A goal without a date of achievement, a dollar amount, expected results, and a written plan, is only an empty wish.**

you want to set a goal of being a quarterback in the NFL.

You could, however, say that you want to create a financial situation that once your children are out of college (assuming you want to pay for it), you'll get a job with the cruise lines teaching ballroom dancing so you can get paid for your cruises and travel.

If you're having a hard time thinking of some of the potential goals, here's a list of some of the most basic, and some that may inspire you to think bigger than ever before.

Some of these will require money to accomplish. Others will require time and commitment and, in many cases, free time requires money.

Please write down all the goals you want on your goals sheet.

Basic GOAL examples:

- Do not run out of money before I run out of life.
- Make sure that my children are taken care of if something happens to me or, if married, both of us.
- Be able to retire before I die.
- Make sure my assets are protected in the event that I'm sued.
- Make sure I have continual income in the event I get hurt or sick and cannot work any longer.
- Make sure I could survive if I lost my job (if spouse lost job).
- Make sure I have a safe source of transportation.
- Make sure I have the right health insurance protection in the event I or one of my children or spouse gets sick.
- Have an emergency fund.

The "I want more out of life goals."

Travel:
- Go and see a live volcano in Hawaii and then, go skiing afterward.
- Go to the top of Mount Haleakala to see the sunrise in Maui.
- Take the mule ride down the cliffs of the Grand Canyon.

121

- Go whale watching in Vancouver.
- Visit three new ski resorts each winter.
- Spend the holidays in a small European village.
- Take a cruise down the Rhine River in Europe.
- Stay in a medieval castle in Germany.
- See the Eiffel Tower.
- Stay in a luxury hotel in Las Vegas.
- Follow the seasons by owning or renting a house in the north for the summer, and the south for the winter.
- Go see the "Running of the Bulls" in Spain.
- Go to Brazil for Carnival.
- Go to New Orleans for Mardi Gras.
- Go to the Rose Bowl for the Rose Parade.
- Go to South Beach, Miami, and find the best shopping and restaurants.
- Take the American-Oriental Express train across the Canadian Rockies.
- Go to Niagara Falls.
- Go to the art shows in Palm Springs.
- Hike the Appalachian Trail.
- Go on the famous 600-mile antique trail through the Appalachian mountain towns.
- Go on an airboat ride in the Everglades.
- Go to Montana and watch the buffalo roam.
- Go on an African safari.
- Go to the Mayan temples in Mexico.
- Go to the rainforests of Costa Rica.

> Sample Italian culture and cuisine by renting a Tuscan villa.

Sports:
> Go to the Stanley Cup Finals.
> Go to the Super Bowl.
> Go to the World Series.
> Attend a major golfing event.
> Play golf at Pebble Beach.
> Play golf at St. Andrews in Scotland.
> Get golf lessons.
> Go to the Kentucky Derby every year.
> Go to the Daytona 500.
> Buy a sports car, join a sports car club, and travel across the country.
> Attend dog shows.
> Would you like to travel to see the Panama Canal?

Health:
> Lose weight — hire a trainer.
> Get a makeover.
> Get massages weekly.
> Go to a hot springs resort and spend a week getting pampered.
> Join a golf or tennis club.
> Go to see a chiropractor monthly.

Spiritual:
> Volunteer at church.
> Visit the Holy Land.

Personal:
- ➢ Join Toastmasters and make a speech in front of a crowd.
- ➢ Learn self-defense (Karate-Tae Kwon Do).
- ➢ Join an acting class.
- ➢ Learn ballroom dancing.
- ➢ Get a college degree.
- ➢ Take an adult education class.
- ➢ Learn how to use the computer better (not so that you can spend more time managing your money!).

Charity:

Give money or volunteer time to:
- ➢ Women's Breast Cancer Foundation.
- ➢ Battered Women's Center.
- ➢ Women's Resource Center.
- ➢ Nature Conservatory.
- ➢ Save the Whales.
- ➢ Animal cruelty.
- ➢ Local schools.
- ➢ A Rotary or a Kiwanis club.
- ➢ My local women's community group, Tangible.

Fun and Recreation
- ➢ New automobile.
- ➢ An RV to travel cross-country.
- ➢ A recreational boat.
- ➢ A vacation house.

Chore Delegation:

- ➢ A house cleaner.
- ➢ A cleaning person.
- ➢ A handyman/woman.
- ➢ A pool person.
- ➢ A lawn care person.

Gifts:
- ➢ Anonymous gift to someone I know who really needs the help.
- ➢ A gift to my children, maybe to help them with their first home.
- ➢ A gift to my grandchildren to help them through college.
- ➢ A gift to my spouse or partner each year to show appreciation.
- ➢ A gift to parents to show appreciation.

Family Time:
- ➢Time to spend with children, grandchildren, or partner.
- ➢Volunteer to babysit for children.
- ➢Time to visit each child or grandchild in different parts of the country.
- ➢A family reunion once a year.

Distribution:
- ➢ Set up my plan so that children will have a certain amount or an annual income after I pass.
- ➢ A certain amount to leave to church or charity.
- ➢ Assurance that spouse or partner will be financially secure and able to maintain the same lifestyle they

now enjoy.

Here's an assortment of other questions to ask that might get your creative juices going:

➢ How close would you like to be to your family?
➢ Would you like to learn to play a musical instrument?
➢ Would you like to learn to act in a play?
➢ Would you like to give money or belong to your local orchestra, drama club, and/or playhouse?
➢ Would you like to sponsor young musicians or actors?
➢ Would you like to learn to fly a plane, a helicopter, a hang glider, or an ultralight?
➢ Would you like to learn how to jump out of a perfectly good airplane — skydiving?
➢ Would you like to learn to speak another language?
➢ Would you like to learn self-defense or even get your black belt?

Lifestyle and Productivity

Lastly, get a job doing something you really want to do, instead of having to do something for the money.

If you're already retired, consider an encore job doing something you always wanted to do but never could because you had to have a job that supported your lifestyle.

I like this goal the best. Have you ever run into someone that they love what they do? I usually meet many of these people in the travel industry.

Imagine that you are so financially set that you can choose the job you want because you love it.

You'll know you have this job when you can't wait to get to work every day.

I hope by now you possess a compelling list of goals. Unfortunately, most people will read this and say, yeah, I'll get back to this chapter and write my goals down later. **Don't do this**!

Stop right now and start writing your goals. Without a comprehensive list of goals and an action plan to get to these goals, you may fall into the common retirement trap.

Goals are important for many reasons. Medical research has shown that people who have goals and an active lifestyle, achieve their goals and live longer.

Having clearly defined goals allows you to enjoy each stage of retirement. The stages of retirement I've observed with most people are:

Stage One is usually immediately after retirement. This is when people do all the things they wanted to do when they were working but couldn't. These things are usually a lot of travel and golf. Once that wears off then they go to Stage Two.

Stage Two is the critical stage because it's either getting into a mundane schedule of just completing errands, or it could be living a whole different level of life.

If Stage One is the euphoric effect stage, then Stage Two should be setting goals and getting started again stage. If you turn Stage Two into the just do errands stage, you are setting yourself up for an early death.

These stages are like you've been on a strict diet for six months and you choose to eat a large cheese and pepperoni pizza.

The first piece tastes the best. If you're anything like me, the first six pieces taste good.

However, if you had to eat pizza every day you'd get sick of it. This is why it makes sense to create a compelling and worthwhile retirement plan. You'll want to have variety and a future with experiences.

If you want to know how to live longer, and have better balance in your life, don't look at retirement as the time you'll stop being productive. The minute you do, that is the minute that you start to die.

When you don't have a larger purpose in life, you'll usually succumb to the commonality of talking about all the negativity in the world, all of which you can do nothing to change.

I love meeting with clients in their seventies who are still working. They work, not because they have to, but because they love what they're doing.

One of your goals could be to become financially set so you can get a job or start a business in something you absolutely love.

The key is to set it up so you can enjoy all the other goals in life. If one of your goals is to travel four weeks a year, you should get a job or business which will allow you to do it.

Most of our new retired clients never considered this as an option. I would suggest you seriously consider this as one of your goals.

If there's any way you can combine some of your goals into a job you would absolutely love and make money at the same time, what could be better in life?

If one of your goals is to give more time and money to the charity of your choice, what's the personal result you would get?

You might answer something like, "I would feel personally fulfilled if I helped someone less fortunate than me."

You might also say, "I feel good because I gave to something bigger than myself."

Lastly, you might say, "I was able to invest my time in something I feel very passionate about."

Your reasons are for you to discover! In the real world, the achievement of a goal means you'll need to give something in return.

If you cannot see the result or the benefit for yourself, most likely you'll not be willing to give something in exchange.

You'll find some things on your list you try to find the result or benefit for yourself but cannot. If after you look at those goals and you say to yourself, "It just doesn't feel right," take them off your list.

Take each of your remaining goals and compare them

against your list of values. If you attain these goals, will they violate your values or will they coincide with your values? If they violate your values, remove them because your values are your guiding path.

Next, write in the dollar amounts these goals will cost you. This is where you get to have fun. Don't guess at the amounts needed!

If you're guessing at any part of this, it's like shooting at a target blindfolded. If your goal is to buy a new car, go and test-drive the car. Get the cost for the exact car you want with the cost for each of the options you want.

If you want to get electric hurricane shutters for your house (this is a big one in Florida), call three contractors and obtain bids. The key with this step is to be as accurate as possible.

You'll find when you work with a comprehensive advisor (coach), they'll expect you to get these costs for your goals.

I'll give you an example. In one case, a client wrote down a new BMW as one of her goals. She went and test-drove the car. She later called me and said she wanted to take the goal off her list. I asked why. She replied, "I always thought I wanted to own one, but after driving it, I actually like my Lexus better. I think I want to put a new Lexus on my list, and replace it every three to four years."

Let me give you one more example. One of my newer clients wrote down they wanted to get involved in a charity. I asked if they wanted to give money, time, or both. They said "just the money."

I wanted them to go and check out a few charities they were interested in. I got a call a few weeks later.

They said they visited the Children's Cancer Center in Tampa, Florida, and were touched by what these children and their families had to go through. They not only wanted to give the money they planned on, but they also wanted me to put in time as one of their goals.

They told me when they visited, it softened their hearts, and neither of them had a dry eye the rest of the day. I absolutely love to see this kind of passion and purpose unveiled once a person gets personally involved in their goals.

The next step involves setting an absolute date for your accomplishment. This is a step where a financial coach may be of help.

Future value calculations will come into play here. My suggestion is to begin by putting down the dates you **would like** to see your goals achieved.

Once you meet with a financial coach, be prepared to adjust some of these dates up or down. You'll see more about how this works a little later in the book. For now, just write down what you think the dates will be.

Some of the dates will be easy if they're based on certain things, such as a minimum retirement age or your children's college education. If you have a ten-year-old and one of your goals is to educate your children, your date for achievement will be eight years away. Make sure you're specific!

Many times clients will plan to retire at age sixty-two. I ask what month and they look at me as if I am crazy. In order to have a real plan you need to know the actual month and day retirement will occur.

When it comes to creating a plan, the actual date in time is very important. If you said age sixty-two, there are 365 days which could be your potential target date.

Goal Prioritization and Compromise.

Leaving this next step out would be like trying to bake a cake and only adding one egg, when the recipe calls for two.

This will be the hardest step by far in your goal-setting strategy. Here is how to think of it... If I had to choose between two goals, would I choose one over the other, or would I compromise on the amount or the date in order to have both?

Before you get started, if you're going to hire a financial coach (retirement planner) you'll need your goals prepared and prioritized.

Before any financial calculations are done, you need a clear idea of what you want as a priority and in chronological order.

In many cases, I've done a plan and found all the goals are achievable and there's no need to compromise. In other cases, there's not enough financial resources, or income, to achieve all the goals.

Here is an example:

Let us say you have two goals—to retire at sixty-two and to fully educate your children through college. If the retirement plan says you have full potential to achieve your goal to retire at age 62, but the cost for college education reduces your chance for retirement to fifty percent, you have to look into making some changes.

One of the changes you can make is to adjust your retirement age. Another is to reduce the amount you want to contribute to the college costs.

If this is the case, you'll need to plan how the rest of it will be paid. Will it be college loans, the child or grandchild working, or potential financial aid do it?

You'll need to compute the financial plan again to see what your potential is.

The objective is to achieve one hundred percent of all your goals. There's no perfect answer! Your answer may be in knowing how to make the adjustments.

As you start on your journey, you'll create milestones to reach in order to attain your goals.

It may require you now have to work another year. It may mean you'll need to contribute less to the college fund, if you wish to retire before age 100. You might have to reduce the amount of your spending today to achieve both the retirement and the college goal. Lastly, you may need to earn more income to achieve your goal.

There are many combinations of plans to reach your goals. The first step is setting the goals. The second is to plan it all out. This is where the financial calculation tool comes into place.

Action Steps:
1) Identify all your goals.
2) Put dollar amounts and deadline dates on your goals.
3) Check your goals against your values.
4) Prioritize your goals as to importance, then by deadline dates.

The difference between where you are now and where you want to be is a plan and the actions to get you there!

ORGANIZE YOUR DATA

After goal setting, your next step in getting your life on track and getting to your financial goals is finding out where you are now.

This is like doing a complete health checkup. When you get a full physical they test your height, weight, blood pressure, blood, urine, EKG, and review your family history.

When you're trying to get your financial future in the best health, you too have to know all your metrics.

In order for you, or your coach, to do this properly,

items to best complete the job need to be known.
- You or you and your spouse's current health.
- Family health history and life expectancy of your parents.
- Children and your relationship with them.
- Do you want any inheritance to go to your children?
- Do you want any inheritances limited?
- Are you concerned with an in-law getting your money?
- How have you made financial decisions in the past?
- When have you gotten worried and had fears?
- When have you felt overconfident?
- When have you lost money?
- When have you made money?
- What have been your best investments?
- What have been your worst investments?
- What do you believe is good or bad? Life insurance, annuities, real estate, stocks, bonds, reverse mortgages, etc.?
- Where do your money beliefs come from?
- Will you make decisions based on your past beliefs or will you depend on the calculations?
- When do you want to retire?
- How do you want to retire — where do you want to live, and how much do you want to spend?
- How will you handle a healthcare catastrophe if it happens? Would you elect in-home or retirement home living? Who would be the caretaker?
- If you lost your spouse, would you live in the same house.

If not, where would you go?

➢ If you opened up your investment statement on a certain month and the markets were down, what amount of volatility would bother you? What is your stress point?

➢ How do you make decisions in your family? Do you and your spouse each have an account for yourselves and then a joint account for operational expenses or do you share all income and expenses?

➢ Is this a first marriage? Are there children from a prior marriage who would be handled differently?

➢ Are there investments you have emotional ties to? An example maybe a stock your father left you or a stock from the company you worked for?

➢ Have you held certain investments because of emotion or fear? If so, what's the attachment or emotion?

If you're going to do it on your own, treat yourself like a client and answer the questions anyway.

Once these qualitative questions are answered it's time to put together the quantitative information.

For an updated list you can go to www.kenhimmler.com/trf/CFQ and download a questionnaire to print out and complete before going to see a planner.

➢ Details on your pension plan. The formula used to compute your pension. Also, the formula used to compute

136

the survivor pension benefits, if you've not yet retired. If you've already retired, your current pension income, is there a COLA, what percent is the COLA, how much in survivor benefits are there, does the survivor benefits have a COLA?

➤ Log onto SSA.gov and print out your most recent Social Security Benefits Statement.

➤ Statements from all investment accounts. It's very important you don't just print the online summary view. This will show only the asset allocation and not the specific security details, the unrealized loss/gain, and the net dividends paid. These are essential factors for the financial planner in determining what to keep and what to sell.

➤ Most recent copies of your latest tax return. It's best if you don't just bring the 1040. In most cases the planner will want to see all schedules. This is where they might be able to save you a lot of money.

➤ Wills and trusts. Bring the full copies, not just a certification of trust. The certification of trust does not show the planner what the distribution method is, whether there's a retirement trust provision, or if the trustee is properly stated with backups and provisions for asset protection, etc.

➤ Any insurance policies and most recent statements. Many times people will bring in just a statement. This does not allow the planner to review policies for items such as no-lapse guarantees, costs and fees, exclusions and pay provisions. Most of the time you'll want to bring in annuities, life insurance, disability insurance, and long-term care insurance policies.

➢ Depending on the breadth of the planner, you might also want to bring in auto, homeowners, health, and liability umbrella policies.

➢ Your goals written out and SMART qualified.

➢ Any business tax returns, buy/sell agreements or entity operating agreements or resolutions.

➢ Any group benefits and booklets from your employer.

Once you have all this information together, get them to your planner *before* your first meeting.

If you don't live in the same city, then either copy and Fed-Ex, or scan and email it to them in advance of the meeting.

If you're worried about identity theft, then blacken out any sensitive data such as Social Security numbers or account numbers.

When you have your initial meeting with a planner you don't want to sit there for the first hour watching them thumb through your data to understand what's going on in your financial life.

From a planner's perspective, I would always rather spend meeting time talking about options, goals and objectives, rather than wasting time data mining and calculating. Even if you're going to go it alone, you will need to assemble all this data.

DECIDE ON HOW TO CREATE YOUR PLAN

At this point you're at the fork in the road. You'll need to ask yourself the question, "Do I do this myself or do I hire someone?" This is a big question and here is what I would tell you.

There's a difference between having the ability to push a button to buy or a sell through an online broker vs. the understanding of how to structure an entire retirement plan with all the complexities that come with it.

Ask yourself, would someone else hire you based on your knowledge and talent in:

❖ Investment research and management.
❖ Trusts, estates, and entities.
❖ Insurance and risk protection.
❖ Tax planning and structure.

If you want to hire yourself, that means someone else would hire you. If this is true, then welcome to the 1% of planners that operate at this level.

If you already know this is not something you want to do, I'll assume you want to hire someone to either do it for you, or to assist you in doing it.

If that's the case, this will be like playing Monopoly.

You get to jump ahead to the Chapter 8, **Finding a Fiduciary Advisor**.

If this is you, then all you need to do is to work on your goals and put your information together. The planner will do the rest.

If you want to do your plan on your own, then please read on. You'll be given step-by-step instructions on how to set this up for yourself.

CHAPTER 4

STEPS TO DO IT YOURSELF

If you're reading this chapter, you've chosen to do your plan on your own. In order to do this, you will need to act as if this is a business — your business.

If you've investigated any businesses, you would've looked at the investment dollar amount, the time, the resources needed, the knowledge or expertise needed, and finally the potential return on your money and time.

This will help you understand what you need to do to properly put your plan together and then manage it. Creating your plan is the same as creating a business.

STEP 1 DEFINING WHAT YOU WILL NEED IN TOOLS-RESOURCES AND TIME

Tools - Resources and Time

Previously, I went through the imaginary U-Inc. This is the company concept we related to your personal financial plan.

In any business, including U-Inc, you need a business plan. Having or getting to TOTAL RETIREMENT FREEDOM means you have a **Plan**.

Hopefully your plan isn't a Napkin Plan but is a fully calculated and stress-tested plan. Napkin Plans are plans in which someone writes out a few figures on a napkin (or if you are an engineer – a spreadsheet) and believes this is a fully calculated plan.

Assuming you're a believer in a fully calculated and stress-tested plan, what tools will you need to create it?

You've heard me talk about being able to do the calculations. This means you'll need to calculate, calculate, calculate, and then compare. You're going to have some heavy calculations to look forward to.

While some of you believe building a spreadsheet is all you need, I'm here to tell you it's not. There's no way a spreadsheet would be able to handle everything needed.

Let me give you an example of what is needed and why a spreadsheet would not work.

➢ You need the ability to input your expenses down to the smallest item. You also want to be able to switch on and off certain expenses, depending on the plan you're going to create. You'll also want to apply separate inflation adjustments to selected expenses. As an example, you want to be able to increase health care expenses at a different inflation rate than housing. You also want to apply different tax outcomes. As an example, your medical expenses have a reduced deduction of 10% based on your AGI.

➢ You need the ability to create different investment models and apply different deviations, risks, and expenses against each model. In addition, each type of account you have may have a different tax outcome based on the type of distribution and profit or loss. This would mean you would have to build the tax code into your spreadsheet.

➢ You need the ability to create different insurance scenarios. You would have to build a spreadsheet that would be able to compare all insurances, homeowners, auto, health, disability, life, long-term care, and umbrella policies. You would have to have the ability to build out different "what if" scenarios of different policies to see the overall effect on your plan. This includes different stress tests such as premature death, health care catastrophe, property losses, etc.

➢ You would have to build a section on how a family trust, a life insurance trust, and a basic will would apply to your situation in your particular state. You would also have to build out a switch to show effects of one person

> IRD is Income in Respect of Decedents. A tax on IRAs and Annuities at death and in addition to any estate tax, if due.

dying vs. the other, if married. You'd also have to program in a switch to have the ability to show death or disability in different years. It would need to be able to compute the estate tax and the IRD tax on annuities and retirement plans in order to play out different tax scenarios. Finally, you'll need to stress test different options and "what if" scenarios.

➤ You would have to have the ability to build out an entire tax "what-if" scenario. This is a necessity to be able to compare different tax scenarios such as:

o Do you do a ROTH conversion? If so, how much and when?

o Do you pay off a mortgage?

o Do you use your mortgage as an offset to tax on your IRAs required minimum distributions (RMD)?

o Do you use a QLAC to reduce your RMD?

o Do you use odd/even year itemized deduction strategy?

o Do you make your charitable deductions from your IRA, or from appreciated assets?

o Do you gift your children now, and which assets are appropriate?

o Do you take accelerated withdrawals from your annuity to reduce the IRD taxation?

o Which account distribution method do you use: low tax, low performance, high liquidity, or high risk? There are up to eight potential combinations that could result in much higher distributions.

➤ You would have to be able to run "what if" risk tests such as:

o Bear market.

o Inflationary changes.

o Tax changes.

o Premature death of either spouse. This gets particularly

complicated because it involves changes in Social Security and pensions.

o   Healthcare or long-term care catastrophe.

Even if someone had the ability to build out this type of spreadsheet, they'd have to create another program which would continually measure and oversee each and every aspect of their plan.

Even if they could do all that, they'd need to build out a plan to automatically download every day, every detail from their taxes, paychecks, insurances, and investment accounts. They'd

> **HIMMLER Rule # 8 Why try to dig a ditch with a spoon when you can rent a backhoe!**

also need a system to alert them if any of these areas got off track.

I think you're getting the idea! There's no reason to try to attempt this when there are tools available already.

Here are the different tools in each area and the approximate costs.

Emoney – Annual Cost $4,800

Emoney is a high end program, best suited for people with more than $1,000,000 or complicated plans.

A complicated plan may be real estate, a business, or a need for heavy tax planning.

This is by far the best planning software I've ever used

and we use this currently in our practice. There is a large learning curve to use properly. It takes up to three months to train a seasoned planner, and up to a year for a newly licensed planner.

Even with that being said, it's by far the most extensive and accurate for all four areas of personal finance: investments, taxes, insurance, and estates and trusts.

It will also cover extensive business planning for death, disability, buy/sell, and selling.

Money Guide Pro – Annual Cost $1,200

In our opinion, this is equally as good as Emoney. It's meant for less complex analysis, and if you have a simple tax situation this will work.

We also use this in our practice and have done so for over fifteen years. We're still very satisfied with all aspects of the program and their service team. The cost is less than Emoney and might be best to start with. The learning curve is less, interface is easier, and the calculations are accurate.

BNA Tax Planner Annual Cost $600.00

This is a necessity to doing the "what if" calculations for the lowest possible tax effect.

PersonalFund.Com Annual Cost $300.00

A necessity for making sure that you are paying the lowest possible fees on your investments.

Morningstar Premium Annual Cost $199.00

A necessity to getting independent investment analysis. You can get the fundamental analysis and, if the investment is covered, the analyst's opinion.

Fundmanager.Com Annual Cost #1,200

This is a PC resident program that is a necessity for testing your portfolio and risks. It allows a correlation matrix to test concentration. It also gives you institutional investment analysis on the fundamentals of the portfolio. You can also use this to test certain asset allocation models.

PolicyCheck.Com Annual Cost $1,200

A web-based program to do full analysis on your variable annuities or variable life.

AnnuityRateWatch.Com Annual Cost $800.00

This is a must in any retirement plan. It allows the sorting, analysis, and back-testing of fixed indexed annuities. Whenever you're building an investment plan that includes annuities, this is necessary as you'll need to compare to bonds. You'll also need to compare one annuity to another. There is a base fee but they do charge each time a back test is done.

WinFlexPro Annual Cost $800.00
Provides a bidding system for your insurances.

HiddenLevers.Com Annual Cost for complete analysis is $11,800 for the scaled down version $3,800
Hidden Levers - provides granular risk analysis on how concentrated you are in each asset category. It will analyze your portfolio as to the concentration into economic lever risks.

As an example: You may have a portfolio that's too concentrated in areas that are affected by currency, oil, retail, manufacturing, etc. It allows you to move these levers to see what would affect your portfolio.

The price is steep, but we feel it's worth it to drill down into a portfolio to understand and reduce its risk. You can buy the watered-down version for a lower price. It will also track and alert you as to changes in the risk levers.

Riskalyze.Com Annual Cost $960.00
This is a risk analysis program based on valuing your risk down to a number. Like a speed sign, it tells you from 25 to 100 how risky you are. It allows you to choose different portfolios based on this easy to select number.

TRX (Total Rebalance) Annual Cost $6,000
Total Rebalance: This will allow you to perform your GAMMA. Gamma is tax allocation, tax swapping, and tax

harvesting.

Estimated Total Cost for Basic Tools - $16,000
(Assumes MoneyGuidePro and not using PolicyCheck, as everyone doesn't have variable annuities or life insurance.)

I know some people who are managing multi-million dollar portfolios who see this as a very small cost to managing their finances.

If you think this is a large cost, then you have to decide on whether it makes sense to outsource the work. I would also do a CEO check on how you view this cost. If you're managing a million-dollar portfolio and you're not willing to spend $16,000 a year on the tools to manage it, you have to question your management attitude.

Remember, the estimates are that GAMMA alone adds in an additional $18,000 a year in returns. This benefit alone pays for all the tools. If you're going to have a successful business, you must have the best tools.

STEP 2 USING THE TOOLS

Part of having and owning a tool entails knowing how to use the tool.

I once had a neighbor who kept a tractor sitting in his backyard. I asked him why he never used it to cut his lawn. He told me it belonged to his son, who only parked it there, and he had no idea how to use it.

He had two acres of grass he cut with a small hand

push mower while a tool that could have saved him his Saturday afternoon sat there unused.

Even if you have the money to buy tools and you learn how to use them you may never know as well as the experts.

Have you ever had the unfortunate luck to break a bone or to even think you broke one and needed an X-ray? As an athlete, I've had too many trips to the emergency room to remember. The process is the same; you wait for five hours to get a ten-minute X-ray and assessment.

My point is if you have enough money you can buy your own X-Ray machine. You could even learn how to shoot your own X-ray film. The real key is, once you shoot that X-ray and put that film on the light board — will you know what you are looking at?

In one instance I had an experience where the doctor put my X-ray on the light board and pointed out a hairline fracture I had in my wrist.

He looked at me and asked, "Do you see this?" To be honest, I was looking right at the same picture but I didn't see at all what he saw.

That was because after many years of medical school, and then years of experience, he could see what I couldn't. I could not identify the fracture; however, I sure could feel the pain, so I knew it was there.

When it comes to money, it's hard for the untrained eye to see the missing money strategies or opportunities.

If you're going to endeavor in this journey on your

own, I would suggest hiring at least for a second opinion.

You would expect to get a second opinion from a doctor if you had major life-threatening surgery.

If you're your own financial planner and manager, why not get a second opinion on your own math? After all, isn't your entire future, your lifestyle, and family's security just as important as your health?

The benefit of you buying the tools and doing this yourself is that you'll probably save money.

The key is not to try to save a thousand dollars by doing it yourself and lose a hundred thousand dollars by missing or messing something up.

If you're dealing with a fiduciary planner, they'll be up front and tell you they don't have a magic formula for beating the markets.

They should tell you as far as returns are concerned, their only goal is to match the returns of the markets.

I have had people come to me for a second opinion and tell me how ridiculous it would be for them to hire this other person, pay them 1%-1.5% a year to only match what they could do by buying index funds.

I remind them that they are not hiring the planner to beat the markets. They are hiring them to take the work off their back, prevent them from making mistakes and finally to find strategies that can add value.

These strategies are GAMMA, distributions strategies, asset protection, estate planning, etc. In most cases the added value from these strategies saves or makes enough to pay for the professionals' time to manage it all

The tools are absolutely needed. If you want to produce your own plan, you'll need to learn how to use these tools and keep up to date on them. It's a business and it needs to be worked just like a job. You'll have to determine if you want this job.

I've been asked what I'll do when I retire. I will surely hire someone like me. I certainly know the amount of time it takes to correctly stay on top of tax, investment, estate planning, and insurance strategies.

For the cost, it's worth it to me to be removed from the labor and the heavy research. This is me — not how everyone sees the world — so for those who want to do it themselves, I commend you.

STEP 3 FINDING YOUR RESOURCES

Resources are the connections and vendors that you work with in any business. Sometimes these relationships are just as important as a good tool.

Certain specialists or even companies can know and inform you of new ideas and strategies. Knowing who is in the marketplace can also save you time and hours of comparative research.

You'll need to put together comparisons of these different resources to assure your efficiency and success.

Here's a short list of the potential vendors you will need

to assemble.

Custodians. Who are the custodians you use for your investment accounts? As an example, TD Ameritrade has totally free accounts, checking, and business accounts. Charles Schwab doesn't have prototype retirement plans (401-A) but has an equity loan program. They also have a fully paid stock loan program. This allows you to loan your stock to short sellers (people who bet against the markets) for very high interest rates. Each custodian has their own positives and negatives. You need to know who to use for each part of your plan.

Insurance Companies. Which insurance companies or brokers do you use? Do you really listen to the insurance agent that comes to your house and sits at your kitchen table? Large brokerage companies are able to run analysis, industry-wide comparisons, and ratings. The other goal is to have a specialist in each insurance area. You'll need to know little items such as if you do put your rental property into an LLC, does your homeowner's or your umbrella now exclude this from coverage? If you have life insurance, who's reading the contracts to make sure there are no traps that might allow the policy to run out of money before you run out of life? I wrote an article back in 2011 with a reporter for the Wall Street Journal. This article covered the thousands of people who have bought life insurance to leave to loved ones or to pay taxes. They have received a surprise that their life insurance may run out before they run out of life. You need connections in the insurance industry to make smart and mathematically correct decisions.

Alternative Investment Sources. Which alternative investments and new options will you employ? As much as I complain about the continual flow of salespeople that send me information, visit our office, or offer us free lunch (oddly enough these sales people know we're not allowed to accept any gift yet they still offer to take me to lunch?) to inform us about new products, they're very useful. Every day, week, and month there are new developments and investment structures and strategies. If you're not on the list of people who get pelted with all this information, you most likely will be left out of the loop! Here is a short list of very recent developments:

o SEC approves online crowd funding for equities.
o Peer-2-Peer lending and equity placement now offers large potential returns and with aggregation, greatly reduced risk.
o Reverse mortgages now have a very low application fee ($125.00) for the line of credit.
o New QLAC rules allow a special annuity to be used to reduce your RMDs by up to 25%.
o New valuation methods create a verifiable way to compare non-traded REIT performance.
401-Ks now have required fee disclosure. If you know where to look you can select the right funds.

Legal and Estate Planning. What lawyers will you use? It's very important to have a good stable of lawyers for each area. You need to make sure you understand how they work, how they charge, and what will they really help you with.

On and on: it's important to stay in the know! The trusted relationships you have in the financial industry are important.

One of the reasons some people make bad money decisions is they trust the wrong people.

This all takes time which is our next step in you making sure you have your plan down correctly.

STEP 4 ORGANIZE AND ALLOCATE YOUR TIME

The amount of time needed to create and monitor your plan must be considered. If you're going to start a new business in your "spare time," you can almost guarantee your own failure.

Warren Buffet was interviewed about his incredible success. He was asked to identify one of the most important factors he could attribute to his success. His answer was, "My ability to say NO." He explained he learned at a very young age he must have one focus.

People who think they can juggle many balls in the air actually do not handle any one of those balls well. For every ball that's in their hand, there are two in the air, out of control.

U-Inc. is no different. If you want to manage your own investments, it's an absolute commitment in time and discipline. For every vacation you take, or when you're away from your computer, your shop's doors are closed. For each hour of missed reading and studying, you're missing out on potential missed opportunities.

You have to have a deep love for what I refer to as the "CHESS BOARD." This is the passion and never-ending desire to win the game. The game is your improvement and protection of your money and future. The game entails understanding how the chess players are allowed to move, and then memorizing every possible move. You'll have to be a master chess player, not only by looking at every possible move, but also five moves ahead. This is being an excellent strategist. It requires a knowledge and continual study of how the game is played.

In the game of YOUR TOTAL RETIREMENT FREEDOM, that means knowing about trusts, estate planning, investments choices, risks and options, taxation, and insurance.

My suggestion is this: if you're in, or nearing, retirement, make an assessment of yourself.

Below is a list of questions you might ask yourself. If you pass, then I'll give you the steps to get educated.

Score each answer between 1 and 5. 1 is I dread it; 5 is I love it.

_____ How do I feel when I read the Wall Street Journal, tax manuals, insurance contracts, and my trusts and wills?

_____ When I wake up in the morning, I can't wait to jump on my computer and read annual reports of the companies I am following.

_____ I enjoy reading investment newsletters, investment books, blogs, and research to make sure I am on track with my investment structure.

_____ I enjoy going to investment conferences, classes, and online webinars.

If your score is:
- Less than 12: Hire Someone.
- Between 13 and 17: Buy your own tools and hire someone to assist you.
- 18 or more: You should definitely do this yourself.

This is a short view but should give you an idea if you are really cut out to run your own U-Inc.

Assuming your score came in above 18 then here are your next steps.

1) Enroll in one of your local college's classes on personal finance.

2) If you're more of a stay at home person, there are high-level classes given by colleges such as the University of Phoenix.

3) Enroll in one of our web-based classes through Kenhimmler.com/trf.

If you would like to know how much time you will need to commit, I can't answer that. It'll be different for everyone and depends on the amount of money you have and the complexity of your plan.

If you have rental properties or alternative investments, then you should plan at least five hours a week after you get your base education. Depending on how big your portfolio gets or the number of rental properties you acquire, you should plan on this being a full-time plus job. That means more than the normal forty-hour week.

Now that you have laid out your time commitment, we're going to delve into your planning tool, MoneyGuidePro.

STEP 5 STARTING MONEYGUIDEPRO

In the last step, we reviewed many different types of software you will need. We're going to start with the planning software of MoneyGuidePro.

This software is going to be able to teach you how to run some of the basic analysis needed to start your Total Retirement Freedom Plan. In this section, we're going to show you the following analyses:

1) Cash flow sustainability.
2) Stress tests:

- ➢ Bear market risk.
- ➢ Premature death.
- ➢ Premature disability.
- ➢ ROTH conversion analysis.
- ➢ Inflationary increase.

If you are still undecided on whether you would like to pay the funds for the tool and do it yourself, then we will give you a trial subscription to MoneyGuidePro. If you would like this, please go to our webpage at www.kenhimmler.com/trf/MGPTRIAL and sign up for free access to MoneyGuidePro.

Disclosure: We do not provide any technical support on your computer, MoneyGuidePro, or financial advice. It will be up to you to learn the program, but you'll get a free trial license to the software.

In the tools section, I talked about Emoney. You may ask, why not use Emoney? Look at MoneyGuidePro like an X-ray machine and Emoney like an MRI machine.

An X-ray can only show you so much. If the X-ray cannot pick up the abnormality, then you're usually sent to get an MRI for a deeper view. An MRI machine is more intensive to run than an X-ray machine.

If you're going to be doing this yourself, I would highly recommend MoneyGuidePro. I believe that a reasonably intelligent person can get the answers they need from MoneyGuidePro.

Here is what I think MoneyGuidePro is good for:
- Cash flow analysis.
- Goal planning.
- Asset allocation and general selection of investment models.
- Determination of need for and amount of life insurance.
- Determination of need for and amount of long-term care insurance.
- Analysis of an annuity income strategy vs. an investment market strategy.
- Bear market risk stress test.
- Inflation risk.
- ROTH conversion analysis.
- Income tax bracket increase stress test.
- Maximum spends analysis to determine what the maximum is that a person can spend without running out of money.

If you have a net investible amount greater than $2,000,000, then Emoney is going to be better suited for trusts, tax planning, and multi-generational planning.

Emoney can do all the items listed that MoneyGuidePro can do, plus it's very strong in the following:

1) Business ownership
- Analysis of selling a business and the options to lowest tax comparisons.
- Selection of entity types between, LLC, S, C, DRE, SP,

and tax comparisons.
- Business shifting and splitting options between trusts.

2) Trusts and entities

We can integrate complex tax planning into a plan to compare different options. The beauty of this is the ability to compare many different types of tax planning options against each other. It compares the tax, but also the net outcome to you and your family. Emoney can compute all of the following tax and trust strategies:

- IDGTs
- GRAT/GRUTs
- QPRTS
- Deferred Gains Trusts (DGTs) (453 Trusts)
- ILIT's Life Insurance Trusts
- Split Gifts
- CRAT/NIMCRUTS/CLT/CRUTS

3) Complex tax analysis

Emoney allows many different tax planning strategies and allows us to compare long term effects of changes proposed. The main tax strategies are:

- Tax Shifting
- Tax Deducting
- Tax Deferring
- Tax Offsetting

4) Cash flow distribution

Emoney allows all the different spend down or decumulation

strategies and allows a comparison to know which strategy to use.
- Lowest tax first
- Lowest risk first
- Lowest performance first
- Highest liquidity first
- Custom: This is my favorite as it allows us to line up all the assets and choose a distribution order to maximize all four of the normal decumulation options.

5) Estate maximization

Emoney allows all the high-end strategies to analyze estate multiplier strategies.
- SOLAR
- Leveraged Life
- IRA transfer
- Annuity and Life Transfer
- Financed Life Insurance

Normally it takes between a year and sometimes three years to train a financial planner on Emoney. Emoney is really not designed to allow a consumer operation.

If you're an MBA or highly skilled at tax, investment, and insurance then you will be able to use Emoney.

MoneyGuidePro, on the other hand, is designed for consumer use and input.

STEP 6 ENTERING YOUR BUDGETS

The assumption is you've logged onto MoneyGuidePro through our website and either bought the program or signed up under our license for a trial.

Whether you've decided to go it alone or to hire someone to assist or do it for you, you'll need to outline your goals.

The following will step through some of the basic questions. Please do this before entering the program, otherwise, you'll spend more time entering and adjusting your goals in the program.

There are three parts to your goals:

1. Survival Budgets

Why do you compute this goal? Many people live in utter fear of losing it all. While fear can be a great motivator it can also be a terrible one.

A basic survival goal might be if a catastrophe hit. You lose your job with no way of getting one back. You or your loved one has a medical catastrophe costing you everything you own. Your house is damaged beyond repair (flood, earthquake, tornado, fire) and the insurance company either does not pay or goes bankrupt.

In this case, you may not receive anything or only the state limit on coverage.

In 1992, people in South Florida lost almost everything with Hurricane Andrew and some of the insurance companies were unable to pay.

I'm sure you can think of many disasters both by nature and by economics. In either case, let's take a look at what you would need as a minimum:

- If you had to sell your house and move to an apartment, what would the rent be? How many rooms would you need and what, as a minimum, could you get along with for food, utilities, transportation, and clothing?
- If you have pets, could you afford to keep them?
- Do you have automobiles you would have to downgrade, or would you have to take public transportation?

I think you're getting the picture. You have to look at the basics and decide if you'll be able to make it in the worst of situations.

I know you might be thinking that the title of this book is LIVE RICH AND STAY WEALTHY. Why then would we take any time at all to figure out survival goals? There are two reasons: the first is to understand the need for certain insurances. The second reason is purely psychological. I truly believe people make bad decisions because of fear. Fear of running out of money, fear of losing money in a bad investment, and fear of needing their money overnight and thus not investing in anything long term.

By understanding what you could live on at a minimum, it helps in making better and more courageous decisions.

164

2. Basic Needs Budgets

These are the basics of what you might need to live on now without some of the pleasures in life.

The basic needs are your housing, food, transportation, children's educational savings, clothing and insurances.
Items such as cable TV, entertainment, dinners out, gifting, charity or travel would be eliminated.

The reason for this is to fully understand what types of investments to make, what insurances to buy, and what your risks are.

Make a list of these basics. If you have upcoming expenses, add them to plan for when you'll need the money. The following is an example only.

If you would like a blank worksheet, please visit www.kenhimmler.com/trf/budget

Housing

Mortgage or Rent Payment	Property Taxes	HOA Fees
HOA Usage Fees	Homeowners/Renters Insurance	Flood Insurance
Earthquake Insurance	Water	Cable TV
Home Phone	Cell Phone	Internet
Electric	Gas	Solar Lease
Lawn Care	Home Warranty	Air Conditioner/Heater Replacement
Roof	Home Improvement	Home Equity Loan
General Home Repair	Pest Control	Pool Service
Home Cleaning Service	Snow Removal	?

Transportation

Auto Loan or Lease	Auto Fuel	Public Transportation
Auto Repairs	Auto Insurance	Car Pool
Auto Replacement Fund	Auto Parking	?

Personal Care

Tennis / Golf	Clothing
Gym / Health Club	Groceries

Home Care/Cleaning	Haircuts / Salon
Massage / Spa	?

Medical

Hearing aids	Health or Medicare Premiums
Eye Glass	Prescriptions
Dental Costs	Co-Pays and Deductibles
HSA Contributions	?

Entertainment/Education

Children/Grandchildren School	Restaurants
Travel	Movies and Shows

Charity

Charitable Gifts

I don't include any income taxes, payroll taxes, or savings to current retirement accounts as it's an expense that will be figured out when you input your income to the program.

3. Wants Budget

While the first part of goal planning is obviously a bit depressing, this section is fun. Before you get started, you'll need to lose your beliefs about what you think is possible.

This has to be what you really want to do with your life. The program and the calculations will help you understand your true potential. You'll never really test your true potential if you don't put it in here.

We're assuming that all your basic needs are taken care of; so this section is all about MORE than the basic goals.

Make a list of the items you might want and assign a cost and timeline to each. Here's a list:

New house	Lawn Care	Full time nanny
Improve your current house	Full time maid	Gifts to church or charity
Gifts to educate your children	Gifts to educate your grandchildren	An RV
International travel	Domestic travel	Anything you can think of!
A second home	New automobile	?

At this point, you should be ready to enter your goals into the software. This step is important so you understand the three different types of goals. For a video demonstration on how to enter these goals please go to www.kenhimmler.com/trf/mgp

STEP 7 ENTERING YOUR QUANTITATIVE DATA

Please do not move to this stage unless you've entered your goals in MoneyguidePro.

Now you're ready to input all the detailed data I asked you to collect in the chapter called **Organize Your Data**.

Most of the information should be very intuitive when inputting to the program. Let me share some of my experience of how people either incorrectly communicate or don't understand how to put in the data.

Homes:

When entering home information here are the specific data you will need.

✓ Purchase date of the home.
✓ Cost basis of the home. Cost basis is the purchase price of the home including closing costs and home improvements.
✓ Mortgage information. Please make sure you have the original date of this mortgage, not any mortgages you might have already refinanced.
  o The outstanding balance now.
  o The current interest rate.
  o Is it fixed or variable?
  o Are you making any additional principal deposits?
✓ The same information for any home equity loans you might have.
✓ Homeowner's insurance statement.

o Note whether you plan on staying in this home or do you plan on moving.

✓ If you were to prematurely die, would your spouse stay in the home (and vice versa)?

✓ If you were disabled, is your house one that you could be cared for in? (One story, stairs, outside, etc.)

Investments and annuities.

For each investment statement, make sure you have:

✓ The original cost basis of each investment.

✓ If a mutual fund, the adjusted cost basis.

✓ The number of shares.

✓ The ticker symbol.

✓ The type of account.

✓ If inherited, the cost basis on the date of death of the original owner.

✓ Beneficiary confirmations.

Insurance Policies

Make sure you have the most recent statement and the policy for:

✓ Homeowner's

✓ Health

✓ Group

✓ Disability

✓ Life

✓ Long-Term Care

- ✓ Automobile
- ✓ Umbrella
- ✓ Business Liability
- ✓ Medicare Supplemental
- ✓ Trusts and Wills
- ✓ Durable Powers of Attorney
- ✓ Health Care Power of Attorneys
- ✓ Living Wills
- ✓ Wills or Pour Over Wills
- ✓ Irrevocable Trusts
- ✓ Revocable Trusts

I'm sure you'll be able to figure out the interface to entering your data but if you want an instructional video please go to www.kenhimmler.com/trf/mgp

STEP 8 RUNNING YOUR SUSTAINABILITY TESTS

The word sustainability can be applied many different ways. In your plan, this is how we define sustainability:

To be able to live in the same lifestyle as you are accustomed to no matter what happens to you by means of an event due to nature, health, or economic disaster.

Another term we will be using which is important to understand is BASELINE — what you're doing right now with no changes. It's where you would end up without any changes.

Here is a very simple BASELINE FACT SUMMARY example.

Age 60, Male; Age 60, Female.

- ❖ Life Expectancy assumption: age 95.
- ❖ Salary: $250,000 a year until age 65.
- ❖ Current annual expenses: $200,000 (Includes your basic needs budget).
- ❖ Current portfolio has a risk rating of 75 (Risk rating goes from 25 to 100 — 100 being the most risk).
- ❖ No life insurance.
- ❖ No long-term care insurance.
- ❖ Married.
- ❖ Neither spouse would move if one died.
- ❖ Neither spouse wants to go into a nursing home, but wants in-home care.
- ❖ Social Security for each spouse is $24,000 a year at age 64.
- ❖ Pension for male is $30,000 a year at full life option, no survivor, and no COLA.
- ❖ No health care benefits from pension or work for either person.
- ❖ Female has a long life expectancy in her family.
- ❖ Male has a shortened life expectancy in his family.
- ❖ Mortgage is a 15-year variable interest rate mortgage with 9 years left.
- ❖ Two children, both married with children.

❖ No goal to leave a certain amount to children. Does not want to decrease life enjoyment to leave a certain amount to children.

❖ Wants to make sure the money stays in the family and does not go to the in-laws.

❖ Wants to provide for grandchildren's education with at least $30,000 per grandchild.

If you're doing your plan yourself, you should create a BASELINE report to double check what you are putting into the tool is correct. All of these facts will be computed with BASELINE projections.

The reason you want to baseline your future projections is once you start adding stress tests, they must be based off the way life is now so you have a point of comparison and measurement.

Using the example above, if you run a stress test showing this particular person's portfolio dropped by 50%, this person cannot retire and may run out of money.

You may also find problems with sustainability for the spouse if one spouse dies with a pension without survivor options that are maintainable.

You'll also find many inefficiency items such as the mortgage, the investment portfolios, and lack of insurances.

By having the baseline plan built, you can run "what if" scenarios to find the right portfolio mix which will allow the growth you need but the risk you can tolerate. You'll also be able to test the plan for insurance needs, tax planning, and risk protection.

We've prepared each stress analysis and you can view how to do this for yourself on our site.
www.kenhimmler.com/mgp

CHAPTER 5

TEST YOUR PLAN

TEST 1 — PREMATURE DEATH STRESS TEST

How do we really know if we need life insurance or not? We calculate, calculate, calculate.

Life insurance is one of those items known to be sold and not bought. A powerful tactic for life insurance agents is to use fear to sell a policy.

In this section, we'll cover whether a person NEEDS life insurance for the sole purposes of protecting an asset or stream of income.

Please don't misunderstand my prior statement. I'm a big fan of life insurance as a leveraging vehicle. This is one of the ways the super-rich got rich; they leveraged. They didn't always use dollar for dollar techniques.

Think about anyone who's super-rich. They've done it through leverage of some sort.

Real Estate Moguls: They've used mortgages and borrowed money. They've made their money on what they're able to net between what they pay on the leverage, and what they collect in rents and growth.

Stock Markets: Many of the billionaires today like Warren Buffet, Bill Gates, and the late Steve Jobs know how to leverage. They let Wall Street attract investors on a leveraged basis to raise funds for their companies.

One of the great ways to use life insurance is to leverage taxes. Your family might owe tax on retirement plans or annuities due to the built-in gain. You can use discounted dollars to pay for the tax. When I say discounted dollars, I'm talking about the death benefit. You may receive $1,000,000 in death benefit and only pay $300,000 over your lifetime in premiums.

It's better to give the $1,000,000 to the IRS to pay your tax debt because you only paid 30% of the total cost.

There are people who have outdated and poor belief systems when it comes to the life insurance decision plans. For some reason, they can't get over their opinion of life insurance and they end up paying dollar for dollar for their tax debt.

Another great way to use life insurance as leverage is to use it to cover long-term care risk with discounted dollars.

In the past, many people would buy life insurance to cover the loss of income, or to pay taxes with discounted dollars.

In 2008, President Bush passed the Pension Protection Act. Since then, you've been able to add a long-term care rider to either annuities or life insurance policies. The way this works on life insurance is you have the choice of either using the total life benefit for either long-term care or as death insurance.

Why would a financial planner like this? We're all about protecting the balance sheet (assets) and sustaining lifetime income. Long term care riders can be a very inexpensive way to cover the risk of premature death or a health care catastrophe.

If your analysis shows that you need long-term care coverage, there are two ways to cover this.

1) **Buy normal long-term care insurance.** This is usually an expensive fix. It requires the person to shell out thousands of dollars a year in premiums. If, by the end of a person's life, they've not used or needed the long term care insurance and passes away, the insurance company wins; they've kept all the premiums and paid out nothing.

2) **Buy life insurance with a long-term care benefit.** This is usually a better alternative but harder to get. The way it works is the insurance company issues a death benefit. If you need that death benefit to pay for long-term care, depending on the company, they will pay between the ranges of 70% to 98% of the death benefit. The other good part is it's currently a tax-free benefit. One of the reasons most financial planners like this is, while not all of us will need long-term care benefits, we will all die eventually. This means the insurance company has to pay back to the family the benefits, whereas with a standalone long-term care policy, they may not pay at all.

With that said, let me give you the caveats.

First, I believe in giving the insurance company the least amount of premium for the highest leverage.

Second, I don't have an opinion on whether term insurance is good or bad. It depends on if your leverage is a long-term play or short term need.

It may be needed for your lifetime for your spouse's income sustainability, or paying a death tax like estate taxes or IRD tax.

If the need is short-term (like covering a debt that will be paid off), term is the better strategy.

Third, I don't believe in holding life insurance in a place that gets double taxed.

Using a life insurance trust to protect the asset and the taxation can prevent this.

You'd be surprised at how many times clients were surprised to learn their life insurance was going to be taxed in their estate. They all say, "But our agent told us the insurance was tax free." I answer back with, "They're right, the life insurance is income tax free, but the death benefit is only tax free as long as your estate does not get taxed."

In many cases, the life insurance itself is what causes the estate to get taxed. This happens mainly due to the life insurance pushing the total estate value over the tax free limit.

This part of the discussion is outside the risk test but I wanted to cover those areas so you didn't immediately say, "Life insurance, I hate that" — or — "life insurance, I would never use that."

For the purposes of running this test in MoneyGuidePro, we're going to show the highest risk, which is dying prematurely in the first year.

This is the highest risk because the surviving spouse would need to live a longer period of time trying to sustain their standard of living.

We will also reduce the current budget by 20%. The normal acceptable financial planning practice says to reduce the expense by 30% for the first to die. I'm going to use 20% to give the surviving spouse a little safety zone.

To learn how to do this in MoneyGuidePro.com please go to www.kenhimmler.com/trf/MGP

When you're done with this analysis you'll be able to determine what need, if any, you'll have for life insurance.

You'll need to go back to your relationships (discussed earlier as part of the tools you need to do your own plan) to get the research and comparisons of what is available for your situation.

Even after you get your bids, make sure you enter each insurance proposal and calculate, calculate, calculate. You will need to compare each bid side by side by entering each one into MoneyGuidePro and compare to see which one works best.

TEST 2 — HEALTH CARE CATASTROPHE STRESS TEST

Now that you've completed the income sustainability tests and the premature death tests, you're ready to see how you fare under the health care catastrophe tests.

What is a healthcare catastrophe?

- Large hospital, doctor co-pay, or deductible not covered by health insurance or Medicare.
- An experimental drug or procedure not covered by any insurance.
- A long-term care expense to cover:
  - In-home partial care.
  - In-home full time care.
  - Retirement transitional community.
  - In-facility full-time care.

These are only a few of the typical health care expenses that can destroy wealth.

The health care issue has always been there but I've found insurance companies are much more selective in what they'll approve today.

These decisions are made in the insurance companies risk management departments. In short, it means if the insurance company can reduce or eliminate payment to you or to the doctor, it's better for their stock price or profit margin.

It might also be better for bonuses and stock options for the people reviewing your case.

With ACA or the Affordable Care Act, we now see reductions in benefits and providers so the masses can have some type of insurance.

Whether you're for or against ACA, its strategy is to spread the costs, which also mean reducing benefits to everyone.

Who will be the big gainers? Those people who could not afford or did not have insurance in the past.

Who are the biggest losers? The young and healthy who are mandated to buy insurance under the law, and the retiree who is dependent on Medicare. Medicare will have to reduce hospital, doctor, and prescription benefits.

Long-Term Care. This is a very interesting area because I 've been around long enough to see a huge increase in the need for this protection.

There's one factor, in my opinion, which has been responsible for the increase in the need for long-term care. It's the computer chip. Why the computer chip?

The computer chip was responsible for the medical computers that discovered DNA and genetics, new drugs, and computer-driven medical devices.

Look at Lasik surgery for eyes; it's almost 100% robotic now. There's a direct increase in life expectancy and the development of the computer chip.

During the turn of the last century, the life expectancy for a male was 45. Now a male in his 70s who does not drink or smoke can expect to live into his late 80s.

If you look back before the super computers were invented (pre-1985), the number of Americans going into long-term care facilities was about two out of ten people.

Today, those numbers are closer to seven out of ten. Thirty years ago there weren't as many choices for extended medical care facilities for seniors. Today, you're able to choose to have in-home care, full-time nursing care, or the new transitional care communities.

Here is how each one works.

In-home care.

Thanks to the computer chip and portable batteries, nurses can come to your home and set up a mini hospital in an hour. If you have certain ailments you may not be fully mobile, or you need supervision. Now you can access this care in your own home without being one of the Rockefellers.

Don't expect to save any money though. From the expenses I've seen from my clients, the cost for in-home, part-time care is just as expensive as full-time in-facility care.

Most people choose this strategy so they can be independent in their own home, and not to be around a lot of other sick people.

Today, of the seven out of ten people who need long-term care, five choose the in-home option.

In today's dollars, the national average cost is $77,000 per year. If you live in Los Angeles, expect to pay on average closer to $104,000. Keep in mind this $104,000 doesn't give you the Four Seasons Hotel treatment, but more like the Holiday Inn treatment.

Full-time care.

This is the normal facility in which you need to live full time for more serious ailments. It might be because you made your daughter-in-law mad. Seriously, I've had many instances that the children just find it easier to put the parents in a home because they don't want to deal with them. The national averages for cost are about the same as the in-home option; between $77,000 and $100,000.

In some cases, it might even make sense to move to another state.

Years ago, a client who lived in Buffalo, New York had been taking care of his father in a nursing home in Manhattan.

It was costing him $125,000 per year. We did the calculations and figured out that his dad's money would be gone in about eight years.

I recommended he move him to a different state. At first, my client thought I was nuts.

I explained that it was an hour's flight from Buffalo to New York City and he could put his father anywhere within an hour's flight and it would not change his lifestyle.

He had no more family in the city, so it wasn't like anyone else went to visit his father.

His father was inside all day and wouldn't know the difference whether he was in Kentucky or New York City.

His father was also not fully coherent. We actually ended up finding an A+ rated facility in Kentucky for $32,000 a year. (That was fifteen years prior to the writing of this book.)

Needless to say, we ended up moving his father to Kentucky. His father ended up passing away after five years. If he would've stayed in New York, most, if not all of his assets would've been spent.

In this case, the entire inheritance stayed intact because we were able to use investment returns to pay for his care.

Transitional communities.

These are communities where you buy a house, equipped with hospital beds, call buttons, direct access to a central building in which nurses and doctors work within the same community.

Typically, you'll start off with a regular house and as time progresses (and if health worsens), these houses become adaptable as private assisted living homes.

In Sarasota, Florida, we helped facilitate this for a client. The house ended up costing him $540,000. A comparable house outside the community would have cost only $300,000.

The reason for the extra cost is they had a deal in which he could move into a smaller house in case either spouse died prematurely.

It also included the costs for the central house, which

housed the nurses and doctors. There was an additional cost of $30,000 per year. This cost covered meals in the clubhouse, the on-site, on-call doctors and nurses, and their annual homeowner's dues. For this additional cost we covered their lifetime risk of medical or long term care. In their particular situation, they liked this living situation and loved the social aspect of the community. They participated in the on-site activities and met many new friends.

I've had other clients who've done this same thing and hated it so much that they lost hundreds of thousands of dollars just to get out.

This is certainly not a decision to be made quickly. Of course you calculate, calculate, calculate. You also need to think through the social and the emotional aspect of changing the way you live, and your culture.

In all three of these options, we don't try to determine which one would be best for you. Sometimes you change your plans, and what you think you would do today may be very different when and if the time actually comes.

For the purposes of computing the plan within MoneyGuidePro, we simply take the annual expenditure of $77,000 per year as the default expenditure needed to cover the risk.

Keep in mind, we're using the budget of your normal living expenses. If you're single, we simply add onto your current budget $77,000 of health care expenses but we eliminate items such as travel, entertainment, etc.

For married people, it gets a bit more complicated. While we find some people say they'll not do the same things they're accustomed to, this hasn't been the case.

When one person in a partnership or marriage goes into a home, the healthy at-home spouse actually consumed more than before. This has sometimes been in the area of travel and hiring help.

Not travel in the normal sense of having fun, but travel back and forth to the nursing home. In some cases, other expenses increase if a new vehicle has to be purchased to accommodate a wheelchair, etc.

In short, we want to keep the same budget for the married couple but add on the additional $77,000 per year. When you're doing the "what-if" scenarios you're going to want to test different ages to compare the risks. If you're going to assume this happens in the future, remember to factor inflation.

In some cases, your plan will show you have no problem paying for this additional expense. The goal here is to protect the in-home healthy spouse.

Therefore, if your plan calculations show the healthy, in-home spouse will run out of money, you'll need to look at insuring this risk.

Of course, you're going to run this calculation if the first spouse becomes disabled, and then you run it again for the other spouse.

Before I get into the next step, let's take a look at one

common mistake people usually make. When trying to insure the risk, most people only look at the long-term care expense lasting three years.

The reason is many people have heard about or read the average time in a nursing home is only 3.3 years. Let me dispel this right now; this is inaccurate. If you Google "how long is a typical nursing home stay, you'll find the average number at 3.3. This comes from studies that use the average time in a facility. The problem with this is the way the government computes the numbers. They use all certified facilities in their study.

In the last ten years, insurance companies have cut reimbursements to hospitals for certain procedures. For these procedures, the hospitals will let you stay for a few days. After your allotted days are up, then you go to a rehab facility. Now rehab facilities are also long-term care facilities.

Let's assume Martha has a hip replacement. She goes to the hospital and has the surgery. The next day, the hospital kicks her out and puts her into a rehab facility, otherwise known as a long-term care facility.

The incorrect numbers are created because Martha's only in the facility for two to three weeks. This two-to-three-week stay is input into the Government's computation, thus averaging down the reported stay period.

In a recent financial planning conference, I brought this problem up at the dinner table with colleagues and we all agreed — the time in a true facility is more around eight to nine years.

My own grandparents on my father's side, were in a facility for twelve years. After the last one died, I remember getting a settlement notice from the lawyer's office informing me there was a negative write-off to their account.

In simple terms, the nursing home bled them dry. The deficit was due to some legal fees the lawyer was writing off as the final expense. The net result: there wasn't a dime left.

The lesson is "do not depend on government statistics to make your plan solid."

Once you figure out the net needed to make sure the healthy spouse is safe, then you'll know how much insurance is needed.

Long gone are the days when the long-term care insurance agent sits at your kitchen table at dinner time putting the fear of Hades in you that you need to buy a huge and expensive insurance policy which you may not need. You now have the number, meaning how much insurance you need.

There are four ways you can take care of this risk.
> Buy long-term care insurance.
> Buy life insurance with a long-term care rider.
> Buy annuities (GICS) with long-term care riders.
> Do nothing.

We're going to explore each way of covering this risk.
The first option is to buy long-term care insurance.

Positives:

- You have a policy where you know exactly what's covered and when. As time goes on and your risk gets less, you can reduce the policy, due to age, your financial term, and risk declines.
- Your policy should have a definition of disability, such as you cannot perform two out of the six ADLs (activities of daily living).
- You only have to pass the medical qualification for long-term care, and not life and long-term care.

Negatives:

- If you pay for the policy for a number of years and then die without going into a home, the insurance company wins. They keep all the premiums.
- Your premiums could increase and most likely will.
- You may have a company that's hard to deal with and fights you on your claim.
- It's very expensive. On average, to cover a husband and wife today, it'll run between three thousand and six thousand dollars a year.

The second option is to buy life insurance with a long-term care rider.

Positives:

- The biggest positive is if you pay the premiums for a number of years and don't use the long-term care part, you'll eventually die and a death benefit will be paid. That is not necessarily a positive; I'm simply pointing

189

out this method allows you to retain the assets. Eventually all the premiums you paid will be paid back to your family, thus not losing money to solve the risk.

- There's a death benefit which is income tax free.
- There's a cash value deposit fund. Depending on how you structure it, you can have liquid funds with a decent rate of return.

Negatives:

- There's no way to get a cost of living adjustment. On a normal long-term care policy, you can opt for a rider that will increase the benefit with inflation. You're buying a life insurance policy with a fixed death benefit and since the long-term care benefit is based on the death benefit, it's fixed.

Some planners will argue with this, saying that you could chose to use dividends and interest on the life insurance policy to increase the death benefit.

I don't recommend this for two reasons. The first is as you get older the cost of life insurance gets bigger. Also, more often than not, the older you get your risk for long-term care costs decrease. The reason is, your life expectancy decreases.

This option will have a negative effect on your cash value. The second reason — my whole philosophy is to pay the insurance company as little as possible.

In order for the death benefit to increase you'd have to either pay the full premiums or overfund the policy, thus giving the insurance company more than absolutely necessary.

- The biggest negative I've seen is this type of insurance is much harder to get. The insurance company is insuring two risks — risk of dying and risk of long-term care. In most cases, if you're applying for just life insurance, ailments like arthritis would not affect the decision of the underwriter, as it's not life-threatening. On the other hand, if you're applying for just long-term care insurance, items such as a heart attack won't affect the long-term care underwriting as much. When you combine both insurances together you're underwriting for both risks at one time.

The third option is to buy an annuity or a GIC with a long-term care rider.

When you buy or invest in most insurance policies, you can add riders. Riders can add on additional benefits which might be important to you. In this case, a long-term care rider is simply a benefit which will activate if and when you need it.

It works like this: You invest $100,000 in an income annuity (GIC). They'll guarantee you'll get 6% income (not return, income) for life or $6,000 per year. The LTC rider says if you cannot perform at least two out of the six activities of daily living, they'll double the income for a period of time. This period varies with companies but it's usually between five to ten years. Therefore, the $6,000 now becomes $12,000 a year in income.

Positives:

- You don't have any medical underwriting. They usually just ask if in the last two years you were in a nursing care facility, etc. This is nowhere near the number of medical questions needed to get actual long-term care insurance or life insurance.
- There's usually no additional cost for the rider or the added protection.

Negatives:

- The only negative I've seen is the annuity rider option does not usually fix the problem.

   Here's an example: Let's assume that Marty and Sue have $1,000,000 in total retirement funds.

   We've done the asset allocation plan and found they should have 30% or $300,000 allocated to guaranteed income contracts.

   This would provide a 6% income per year or $18,000.

   We then complete the risk analysis of the health care problem. We find if one of them has a health care catastrophe they're still in need of $77,000 per year.

   The rider on the annuity/GIC would double the $18,000 to $36,000.

   They're still short by $41,000. This is a negative

because we cannot choose the amount of the insurance on the annuity because it's a function of how much we have invested and the rider payouts.

On a positive side, it does mean that if Marty and Sue were going to use Option 1 (buy regular long-term care insurance) or Option 2 (buy life insurance with a long-term care rider) we might be able to buy less insurance as we have some coverage through the annuity.

At this point, you are probably wondering why your long-term care insurance agent never told you this.

The fact of the matter is the insurance agent is not a financial planner. To expect this type of advice and calculation is like expecting champagne from squeezing lemons.

The fourth option is to do nothing. I'll bet you were expecting me to tell you how crazy you would be to do this, or how much risk you might take on.

Actually, there are many cases in which we've instructed clients not to buy long-term care insurance or to get rid of the policies they currently owned to save the premiums.

The reason they bought the insurance was usually emotional without the benefit of the calculations. We've found people who could've added $140,000 in additional expenses for long-term care every year and they still wouldn't run out of money.

They owned and were paying thousands for long-term care insurance, and for what? They were sold the policy out of fear. When we proved to them even if both of them needed long-term care they would never run out of money, most of the time they're flabbergasted.

In other cases, we've told people to either cancel the insurance or not buy it because we had computed the premiums for the insurance would actually cause them to become financially unstable. Paying a large expense for insurance can drain your future financial stability.

If your financial plan shows you're close to running out of money, you'll need to get into defensive mode and start saving money, not spend more on insurance premiums.

I actually had a dentist hire me. After I constructed the plan, I found he was paying 24% of his annual income in insurance premiums.

This was because, in his Jewish community, there was a very good insurance salesman who put the fear of poverty in everyone in their community. He also didn't want to say no to the insurance salesman due to the social tension he thought it might create.

After I showed him that his insurance premiums would make him have to work another ten years, he agreed to reduce the policies and premiums.

Here are some tips on long-term care insurance if you're going to use it.

- Take a longer waiting period; the longer the waiting period, the lower the premiums.
- Make sure you have a cost of living increase rider.
- Make sure it covers both in-home and nursing home.
- Check the definition of need. If only two out of the six failures of activities of daily living are needed, then it's normal. If it's more than two, then shop around.
- Check to see if you have group coverage through your work or an association you might belong to. This will usually be less expensive.
- See if your state has a partnership program as that might also reduce your premiums or offer premium refunds.
- Don't buy into the sales pitch that it's tax deductible. While technically it is, most people cannot exceed the 10% floor on medical expenses to actually save money on taxes.
- If you do deduct the premiums, be very careful to know the ratio of deductions and if it's qualified or non-qualified. A tax penalty with interest can wipe out years of savings.

If you're going to use life insurance with long-term care benefits, then:

- Make sure you read the provisions of the payouts. How much of the death benefit can be used for long-term care?
- Can it be used for both home health and facility or just facility?
- Make sure you have a no-lapse lifetime guarantee. This

means if the policy internal rate of return does not perform to what the insurance company originally projected, they cannot cancel your policy nor can they increase your premiums.

➤ If you have an estate that is near or exceeds the current estate tax exemption, make sure you buy the life insurance inside of its own life insurance trust. (Otherwise known as an ILIT).

➤ If you have a joint or second-to-die life policy with a long-term care rider make sure the long-term care can be activated on the first person to become disabled. Most policies do not pay the long-term care until the first person dies. This means that you might be thinking you have long-term care insurance when you really don't.

TEST 3 — INFLATION RISK STRESS TEST

Hyperinflation has been a fear of anyone in their retirement years. If you look at what a Cadillac cost in the 1950s (around $5,000) and what it costs today (over $50,000) inflation is a real risk to the retiree.

Don't expect any help from the government. It will continue to reduce the published inflation rate because it's self-serving.

People who are in their twenties or thirties have not lived through hyperinflation, so of course they're not going to be as concerned about it as the retiree.

When you're retired and inflation goes up by 6% but

your investments, Social Security, and pension only go up by 2% that's a real problem. You're on a fast path to running out of money. You'll have to take more and more out of your principal each year just to have the same lifestyle.

The only way to plan for inflation is to earn more after tax than the inflation rate, and reinvest the difference.

TEST 4 — TAX INCREASE RISK

Our national debt is 19.5 trillion dollars and growing at 3 million a minute. This means that every American owes $55,000 to the debt load. If anyone thinks income taxes can go down, they'll need to replace the batteries in their calculator.

The bottom line is if you have a large amount saved in before-tax accounts such as 401-Ks, pension plans, IRAs, 457s or annuities, then you're in the risk pool. You'll be required to take money out of these accounts at age 70.5 and will force taxable income.

What happens when they increase tax rates? It means less income for you. This analysis must be run to see what the impact is on your sustainability.

If you've been one of those people who has saved the majority of your savings into these types of accounts, any tax changes will affect you drastically.

If, on the other hand, a majority of your money is in real estate or after-tax investments, the impact should be much less.

In either case, you need to run this analysis to see how this will impact you.

When you're in MoneyGuidePro you'll simply go to the settings and use a "what if" scenario to show an increase in the tax rate.

When I run this analysis for clients I like to use three levels.

> ➢ Level 1 is using the current brackets.
> ➢ Level 2 is increasing the tax by 10%.
> ➢ Level 3 is increasing the tax by 20%.

In all of these scenarios you can get a better idea of where your weak points in your tax plan are. To learn how to do this in MoneyGuidePro.com, please go to www.kenhimmler.com/trf/mgp

TEST 5 — BEAR MARKET RISK

At this point you should have learned how to understand your investment risk. Now we'll test to see if you could survive during a short-term market crash.

We're going to use a two-year bear market with a 20% slide the first year, and another 20% slide the second year.

Additionally, we're going to test this in the first two years. Why the first two?

The first years are the riskiest in your retirement because of compound interest and the number of years you have left. In financial planning terms this is called an unfortunate sequence of returns.

This tip is important because you'll need to know your tool.

MoneyGuidePro has an odd way of computing market risk. In their Bear Market stress test, you can put in what the drop in the market is; but the program figures out a new rate of return thereafter to average out the returns over time.

To me, it's not realistic if you're retired and need cash flow from your portfolio.

We like to take a more drastic and conservative approach. We'll be assuming there's a 20% market drop each of the first two years and then there's no return to the average. To do this, we'll bypass their tool and create a workaround.

We'll be inputting this drop in the market as an expense equal to 20% of the portfolio in each of the first two years. In order to compute correctly we need to tell the program not to take it out as a taxable event. Normally, a large expense is viewed as buying something.

Using this workaround will reduce the portfolio just like a bear market, but does not allow the portfolio to make up for the losses by increasing the return.

What about using a Monte Carlo analysis? This is a common tool used by some financial planners. It's supposed to run thousands of simulations of market ups and downs.

It determines statistically if your plan will succeed. This is again a lesson in knowing your tool. Depending on which software you use, you can get drastically different results. Some programs that have a Monte Carlo simulator do not assume negative cash flows, income taxes and inflationary rates. Some programs also use different models to determine the sequence of the ups and downs.

It's all a guess and you really have to look under the hood of the program to know how they're computing the numbers.

One of the reasons I don't like to use the Monte Carlo simulator is it's based on a random sequence of losses and gains.

If the sequence of the losses occurs at the beginning of the period, you could run out of money.

If the sequence of losses occurs in the middle or the end of the plan, it's much less risky due to the shortened period of time the portfolio must sustain your cash flow.

A Monte Carlo simulation uses the average of the up and down sequences. It will then return a potential success rate.

In financial planning circles, it is thought to be acceptable if the success rate is above 90%-92%. The problem is if you retire right when the market goes into a two to three-year crash, statistical averages will not mean anything.

This is why I like using an actual loss of the market in the beginning years to simulate a bad sequence of returns. You cannot manipulate a Monte Carlo simulator to do this so you have to use a different method to do the stress test. To watch this analysis and how to run it yourself, you can go to http://www.kenhimmler.com/trf/mgp

TEST 6 — TRUE INVESTMENT RISK

What is investment risk and how do you measure it against your cash flow and sustainability? Let's outline the different risks you may encounter.

Inflationary Risk

This is the loss of the purchasing power of your money because you've not kept up with inflation after tax.

Tax Risk

Tax risk is the risk the government increases the tax rate on a certain investment type or category. As an example, just recently, the government imposed an income-based penalty on Medicare. If you've saved a lot of money into a retirement plan, this may cause forced taxable income which can trigger the Medicare Penalty.

Volatility Risk

Volatility risk is only considered a risk under two conditions. The first is emotional response. This means that you take a buy or sell action on a portfolio when portfolios go up or down. People buy when prices are high and they sell when prices are low because they respond to greed or fear. The second condition is when someone needs income and they have a volatile portfolio. When the portfolio is down they have to sell investments at a loss to produce cash flow. If the portfolio is designed correctly around the cash flow, volatility risk should not be present, setting aside the emotional response problem.

Loss of Principal Risk

This is most commonly confused with volatility risk. When asked, most people will define risk as when their account goes down. Loss of principal risk is activated upon two triggers. The first is the same as volatility risk — emotional response. The second is when the actual investment is lost. This risk can be greatly reduced by asset allocation and diversification. If you're in the habit of buying single stocks, single bonds, real estate projects, or other single issue types of investments, you run a higher risk of loss of principal. 5)

Opportunity Risk

Since 2008 and the Great Recession, I've seen more money in cash and money markets than ever before. This most likely is out of fear or a lack of knowing what to do. Opportunity risk is when you have two similar risk investments, but one is paying much higher than the other. As an example, if I have a bank money market account paying .25 and I also have a fixed liquid annuity paying 2.50% there's an opportunity loss of 2.25%. While this may seem like a very low number, it amounts to $2,250 on every $100,000 you have invested, or should I say *don't* have invested.

Investment Concentration Risk

Earlier, I talked about having too much concentration in one stock. This is a risk that goes against all fundamental investment mechanics. There are, however, those people who have worked for companies and put all their savings into their company's stock and have done well — until they didn't. There are too many cases where companies are downgraded, bankrupt, or the price simply slides due to global economics. You could subject yourself to concentration risk through mutual funds. Mutual funds, while they're supposed to be diversified, are still run by a manager. This manager has a philosophy or strategy. This is a personality trait or a human pattern of how to buy and sell in the markets. A manager may set certain sell triggers, buy triggers or be concentrated in value, growth or emerging types of investments. By owning only a few mutual funds, you're still susceptible to a higher risk than a fully diversified and allocated indexed portfolio. All of these factors make up investment concentration risk.

Category Concentration Risk

Much like its relative, Investment Concentration Risk, or over-investing in one category, can also create devastating results. Remember, asset allocation is when you have assets positioned in different categories with the intent of having those categories offset each other with the ups and downs. We commonly get new clients who either hired money managers or tried to do it themselves without the proper tools and are too heavily concentrated in categories. An example may be someone who has an S&P 500 fund or ETF, a Russell 2000 fund or ETF, and a Wilshire 5000 fund or ETF. While you might think you're safer because you're fully diversified, you're not. Your risk is most of the investments within these categories run lock step with each other. While some may argue that the Russell will not follow the same trend as the S&P 500, they'll both still go down when the overall market goes down. One may go down more than the other, but they're still both going to tank at the same time.

Now that you've been fully educated on all the risks the next step is to take the tools you purchased (from the chapter on tools) and start computing your risks.

Once you've identified your personal risks you'll be able to remodel the risks when we get to Chapter 6 - Deciding What Changes to Make. The tests you will run for yourself are:

- ✓ Position Concentration Risk
- ✓ Positive Correlation Risk
- ✓ Volatility Risk
- ✓ Fundamental and Quality Risk Analysis
- ✓ Position Overlap Analysis
- ✓ Category Overlap Analysis
- ✓ Opportunity Risk Analysis

TEST 7 — REDUCING INVESTMENT FEES

Any retirement plan must include an analysis of investment fees.

> ➤ On average, a variable annuity may charge between 3% and 4.5%.
> ➤ A typical large cap domestic mutual fund may charge on average 1.5% -2%.
> ➤ An international or small cap fund may charge upwards of 2.5% per year.

On average, if a mutual fund charges 1.5% and they have at least a 50% turnover expect another 2% in internal, non-reportable costs.

That's a total of 3.5% for the privilege of investing in a mutual fund that statistically will underperform the markets.

In many cases, a company that sells mutual funds may also manage funds. This is a large increase in your fees so let's add them up.

➤ Mutual Fund Fee	2%
➤ Management Fee	1.5%
➤ Total fees	3.5%

When the average return on equities has only been hovering around 8%-9%, you cannot give up 30% of your gains back in fees. What would a reasonable fee to pay be? It depends on the actual services you're getting. In either case, it should not exceed 2%.

In your analysis, you're going to look at changing certain investments in order to reduce the amount of fees.

It could be moving mutual funds to individual stocks with an index type of strategy. It could be moving variable annuities to fixed index annuities.

The goal is to use the most efficient vehicle with the least amount of risk and cost to get you to your destination.

To learn how to do this in MoneyGuidePro.com, please go to: www.kenhimmler.com/trf/mgp

TEST 8 — CALCULATE YOUR WANT BUDGET

I'm assuming that you've run your baseline goals against max spend sustainability and all the stress tests. If you've computed this and you've succeeded, then it's time to see how far you can go.

The key to running the same analysis against the WANT GOALS is to play with different areas in your expense and goal sheets.

As an example, if you've put down to spend $50,000 a year in travel, what happens if it doesn't work?

Keep reducing the amount until you get to a place where you have an acceptable and workable plan. You're simply going to take your Want Budget Worksheet and create a separate "what if" scenario to see what you're capable of.

If your plan is not sustainable under this new budget, then reduce the budget in small increments until you can see what your maximum capacity really is.

To learn how to do this in MoneyGuidePro.com, please go to: www.kenhimmler.com/trf/mgp/maximumspend

CHAPTER 6

DECIDING WHAT CHANGES TO MAKE

Now that you've gone through and run your cash flow sustainability and your stress tests, you should be able to answer the following questions:

CASH FLOW SUSTAINABILITY

➤ Will you be able to maintain your cash flow and portfolio value, **assuming there are no changes** to your income or expenses, with no added stress?

➤ What's the maximum cash flow you can spend without running out of money? Answer this question for each of the three budgets.

➤ Do you have a zero-end plan, a fixed-end plan, or a flexible-end plan? Depending on which type of plan you're using, have you decided on a balance between what you want to spend and what you might want to leave to someone else? This is done in the "what if" modeling.

Zero-end plan. This assumes you're willing to spend all your money. At the end of your plan (in other words your life expectancy) there's very little or nothing at all.

This assumes you would rather spend your money than to leave it to someone else. This is also sometimes called a max spend down plan.

Maybe you've seen the bumper sticker that says, "When I die I want my last check to the funeral home to bounce." Or the one that says, "I'm spending my kid's inheritance."

Fixed-Sum End Plan. This assumes that you want to leave a certain amount of money to children, grandchildren, or a charity.

Flexible-End Plan. This assumes that it doesn't matter to you if there is anything or not. You are going to spend the amount you're comfortable with. If there's anything left then great; if not, oh well!

PREMATURE DEATH

What happens if you're married and one of you has a premature death? Have you done the calculations both ways? In other words, what happens if you die first and then what happens if your partner/mate/spouse dies first?

If this stress test does have the possibility that you may not have sustainability, then have you considered and calculated different scenarios to fix it?

LIFE INSURANCE

Compare all types of insurance. Term, whole life, universal life, and equity indexed life. How will you pay for it?

✓ Can you set up a 401(A) to get a deduction on the life insurance or use a 412(e)3?

209

- ✓ Can you improve an old life insurance policy to get a higher amount?
- ✓ Can you use your IRA to pay for the life insurance with a SOLAR plan?
- ✓ Can you use an annuity to pay for the life insurance?
- ✓ Calculate using other assets such as a reverse mortgage.
- ✓ Calculate a change in your or your spouse's lifestyle to adjust for the other's premature death.
- ✓

HEALTH CARE CATASTROPHE

What is the result of one or both of you having to pay out between $77,000 and $125,000 a year in additional expenses? If a long-term care expense creates a risk against your sustainability, have you considered and calculated different scenarios to fix it?

- ✓ Calculate buying long-term care insurance in MoneyGuidePro.
- ✓ Calculate buying life insurance that has a long-term care rider that allows you to use the death benefit to pay for life insurance.
- ✓ Calculate using an annuity with a long-term care rider to cover some or all of the shortage.
- ✓ Calculate using a Section 105 to pay for the expense to reduce the cost by tax deductions.
- ✓ Calculate fully funding an HSA to pay the premiums later in life.

- ✓ Calculate using a medically underwritten annuity to co-fund the coverage.
- ✓ Calculate what would happen if you used a reverse mortgage.
- ✓ Calculate selling your house and moving to an apartment.

INFLATIONARY INCREASE

What's the result of inflation increasing and your money not keeping up? There are certain asset classes which will get hurt and certain ones that will not. As a note, as of the writing of this book we're using a base rate of 3.73% in our calculations for clients.

- ✓ Calculate in additional increments of 1% increases in inflation and what happens to your sustainability. Do you have any investments that would perform well if inflation increased? Investments such as currency hedges or TIPS are only a few.
- ✓ What adjustments would have to happen to your cash flow, and at what point in an inflationary increase would you have to start to make expense reductions?

The key is to head off the accelerated spending before you run out of money.

TAX INCREASE

What happens if you increase the overall tax rate or just the retirement tax triggers?

- ✓ Calculate your required minimum distributions and what that does to your adjusted gross income (AGI). Do you jump to another bracket?
- ✓ Does this increase your Medicare premiums with the new income-based penalty?
- ✓ Do you lose any of your Schedule A itemized deductions? *This means that you would either lose or get a reduced deduction on your medical, property tax, mortgage interest, charitable deductions and all miscellaneous deductions.* Calculate a general increase in tax brackets going up. We like to use increments of 10% above the current brackets. What happens to your cash flow and your sustainability?
- ✓ Calculate the tax difference if you did tax allocate your investments by putting the capital gain assets into your non-retirement account and put the ordinary income assets into the retirement account.

BEAR MARKET

It is important to make sure you do not create an urge to make an emotional investment decision. You do this by understanding your risk tolerance. Calculate what happens when you take a 20% loss in the first year of your plan?

- ✓ Does this change your sustainability?

- ✓ Does this require you to make some changes in your lifestyle?
- ✓ What happens if you take a 20% loss in your portfolio every seven years? (The average occurrence of Bear Market crashes).
- ✓ If a down market will change your sustainability, then calculate a change in the portfolio asset allocation mix. What is the right mix to maintain your sustainability? Also remember that, when you are reviewing asset allocation models, the standard deviation is only the average up/down. Find the worst and best year analysis on the asset allocation model. If you have a standard deviation on a portfolio of 12%, that only means the average up/down is 12%. It may have lost as much as 25% to 40%. How long did this downturn last?
- ✓ Could you leave that portfolio alone and have cash flows come from other places until the portfolio regained its losses?
- ✓ Can you change the model to a less aggressive one? If you're in a position where the bear market crash stress test does not affect you, can you move to a higher target model with more volatility and not affect your sustainability?

TRUE INVESTMENT RISK

Understanding where you might have risk hiding is important to improve your overall performance. If you have an asset allocation plan, this will help you reduce risk.

But it's best if you also know the factors within that allocation model that may pose a problem.

✓ Calculate what the actual risk is as it applies to each category and weighting.
✓ What happens when one part of the economy goes down? Does this adversely affect your investment portfolio or do you have a well-balanced plan?
✓ Can you move certain categories into less risky or volatile areas while still keeping the same targeted rate of return?
✓ Calculate moving some (or all) of your bond allocations to fixed indexed annuities with income riders.
✓ Calculate moving some (or all) of your equity allocations to fixed indexed annuities that have high or no caps on the indexes.
✓ Calculate moving some (or all) of your personal real estate holdings into liquid marketable REITs but diversify the categories. As an example, if you have ten residential rental properties, can you sell three or four and move that equity into senior housing, student housing, health care, or commercial? These sub-asset

classes of real estate will usually have different risk levels and volatility in downward real estate markets because of their tenants and economic stability.

- ✓ Calculate moving concentrated single-stock positions to ETFs that have better diversification.
- ✓ Calculate insuring stock or ETF positions with protective puts. While you may give up some of your returns to pay for this insurance, it may be the only thing that allows you to sustain your lifestyle through an economic downturn.
- ✓ Calculate selling covered calls on your portfolio to develop more income and look to use that income to live on, or reinvest in other categories to diversify away from concentrated risks.

If you own concentrated positions in stocks or businesses, calculate using DGTs or 664 trusts to wash out the tax to allow you to diversify. We see a lack of people using this technique when someone retires from a company that has given them company stock.

You want to reduce your risk of holding any position in an over concentrated manner.

If people didn't learn the lessons from those people that owned MCI, Enron, Puerto Rico Bonds, Orange County Bonds, and others, they're doomed to run the same risks and possibly live it all over again, or should I say *lose it all* again?

REDUCING INVESTMENT FEES

It's impossible to get away from fees. You'll have to pay something to manage your investments.

Warren Buffett says, "It is not what you pay but the value of what you get."

Value is not defined by a promise of high returns. Remember, no one can control returns. You can however control the net take home pay of the returns you do get.

Certain clients have told me some brokers have said the higher the fees the better returns; that's a bunch of *you know what.*

> You can go to www.kenhimmler.com/trf/gamm a to learn more on how to increase your net returns without increasing the risk.

✓ Calculate what you could save by changing the methodology of how you invest. This is a very tricky area to calculate correctly.

If you're paying a mutual fund 2% and a manager 1%, you're paying a total of 3%.

On the other hand, if they're acting as your trustee, doing your tax returns, doing all of your financial planning, and paying your bills then you have to compare the value of what you're getting.

Usually, we find many of the brokerage firms charging

the 3% are only doing the investment management.

You want to look to reduce fees and increase the service, value, or what we refer to as GAMMA.

CHAPTER 7

IMPLEMENTING YOUR PLAN

You've completed your stress test and your calculations to make comparisons. You're now ready to put your plan changes into place. The question is: Where do you start?

While you can pick any place to start making changes, look at this like remodeling a rental property. You'll need to replace plumbing, electrical, drywall, and the kitchen. You want to do this as soon as possible because the longer you wait, the more you lose in rental income.

You start with the mechanical parts of the home such as the plumbing and electrical. If you start with the drywall, you may be replacing it again if you find you have to replace more than originally planned.

In your TOTAL RETIREMENT FREEDOM PLAN, you want to start with your investments.

Your investments are going to drive your entire plan. They'll pay for your cash flow, your insurance, and drive your taxation. Here's a step by step process of what to change first. Keep in mind there could always be reasons as to why you might not do them in this order but you have to have a process to start with.

INVESTMENT CUSTODIAN

Are you going to keep your money with a high-priced broker or are you going to move to a discount broker?

If it is a discount broker, which one do you use or do you use multiple ones based on what you want?

As an example, Schwab has an equity loan program that you can borrow against your funds like a home equity loan. They also have a program which allows you to loan your stocks to short sellers and potentially earn a very high rate of return. This only works on certain types of investments, but can be very profitable.

TD Ameritrade has a program with about 100 ETFs that you can trade free.

Once you pick the best place for you, the action is to contact that company. Let them know you want to roll your accounts into their company. They'll send you the forms and once you complete them, you'll have about two weeks ahead of you.

In this transfer process, you'll also want to make sure you're titling your accounts correctly.

If you have retirement or annuity accounts, those also need to be titled correctly and you should keep a copy of the signed beneficiary form.

Many of these companies will ask you to fill out everything and sign on the dotted line. That's fine, but then you should keep a physical copy of the beneficiary designation form.

INVESTMENT RISK REDUCTION

Once your funds land at the new company, it's time to get to work.

You should have your account correctly set up with the right beneficiaries. Now start trading to get to your asset allocation model.

If you have investments with high gains built in, you have to go back to your tax tools you purchased to weigh the tax load.

You can wait and spread out the tax gain over a period of time, but it must be weighed against the risk of the investment possibly going down.

This potential risk has to also be weighed against what you learned in your analysis regarding how much risk your plan can really sustain.

You can either buy a PUT on the investment to reduce the risk until the next tax year, or just bite the bullet and pay the tax.

Many times, clients don't want to sell an investment because of the tax. If the investment drops, you'll have wished you could go back and just pay the tax.

TAX STRUCTURE

You might be asking if the tax structure should come before the investment risk reduction. In most cases, your tax structure is done before you get to the investment risk reduction, so you already know where you're going to place certain investments.

Tax structure mainly pertains to items such as ROTH conversion, saving to before- or after-tax vehicles, to set up a retirement corporation, to use a 401(A), HSA, 105, which investments to place into which accounts or other tax structures previously discussed.

INSURANCE CHANGES

That feels good to get all the investments into the right place, right? Your next step is to start the bidding process of the insurances to see what you can do to improve your protection.

You should have completed the risk analysis to understand which insurances you need, and whether to change the deductibles, waiting periods, coverage, and owners. You also know if you need any additional insurance.

In this bidding process, you're also going to overlay your tax structure.

As an example, if you set up your retirement corporation, are you going to pay for your health insurance and long-term care insurance through it?

If you're setting up a 401A, are you going to pay for

your life insurance through it?

Are you going to use a 412(E)3 to pay for the life insurance? Hold on — before you make your changes to the insurance — you have to complete Step 5.

TRUSTS AND ENTITIES

Whether you're creating your first family trust, or amending your current one, you'll always need a plan.

If you're creating a life insurance trust or a deferred gains trust, this is also where you start.

If you're creating or using a retirement corporation or LLC, here's where you're going to begin.

If you're creating new trusts or entities, you're going to go back to the investment accounts and any other assets and change the titles and/or beneficiaries.

This step is also where you'll change the insurances to the new trusts or entities.

Be particularly

> For an Estate Plan checklist and education on trusts go to
>
> kenhimmler.com/trf/fpp

careful if you own rental properties and you have placed them into an LLC or corporation.

Your typical homeowner's policy may not cover it as an entity. You also may need a review of an umbrella policy.

Whew! You're finally done remodeling your financial

future. Just like the rental property example, you'll now need to get it into management mode. On to the next step!

> If at this point you've lost interest, fallen asleep or would've rather have watched bowling on TV, then doing your plan yourself may be a mistake. You have to love this stuff to be good at it and stay at it. Consider hiring

MEASURING AND MONITORING

Your next step in the process of getting your plan created is to have an automated structure to allow your plan to be managed after you put it into place.

Your TOTAL RETIREMENT FREEDOM PLAN is a living, breathing, and ever-changing plan. As soon as you create it, it will change. Why?

- Every day, the value of your investments changes.
- Every day, you get older.
- Your income can change.
- Your expenses can change.
- Your goals should evolve and change.
- Your family may change.
- Your health may change.
- Inflation changes.
- Congress adds in an average of over 450 new tax laws

223

every year.
- Your job may change.
- Your local economy may change

I don't think I can state all the potential changes that could affect your plan.

The one fact I can state is you need to automate your plan. This is so you don't need to be the one building and modifying spreadsheets daily to follow all the changes.

Some of the calculation tools I mentioned in the last chapter have the ability to automate your entire plan in the ongoing management task.

As an example, MoneyGuidePro and Emoney can totally automate the entire plan for you.

Emoney even has an alerting system which will tell you when your plan gets off its original track.

Some of you may be familiar with the semi-automation program from Intuit called Quicken. It will download your

> That which is not measured cannot be managed. That which is not managed will soon fail.

checkbook, savings accounts, and investments. This is what I call partial automation. The full automation solutions are through the calculation tools I mentioned before.

At this point, I should give you a disclaimer. I don't work for, nor do I own stock in, any of the tools I mention. I continually promote them because I know how they will help someone.

The key is to create a system that works on its own. If you must continually spend time inputting data and then massaging it, then you're not being a very good CFO.

CREATE A MAINTENANCE SCHEDULE

If you want to personally manage your finances, you should hold yourself to the same standard as a professional.

This is always a sensitive area. No one likes to be told they're not doing a good job, even if they're guilty of it.

That may be one of the reasons that people hate to jump on the scale, especially after the holidays. It's an instant gauge to report on your discipline of eating.

Sports teams have scoreboards. Employees have reviews. Financial planners have report cards.

If you're going to manage things yourself then you should have a schedule, a list of deliverables, and strong sense of accountability.

If you cannot do this, then it is time to hire someone else. Even when you hire someone else you must have a clear vision of the professional's responsibilities.

The following Calendar Quarter Maintenance Tasks are needed to keep your plan on track.

Grade how well you do on each one. You'll use grades just like you would in school. Grade with a percentage based on if you did it well, you did it on time, and you did it efficiently.

NOTE: In your report card you're not expected to check into your investments daily, monthly, or even quarterly. If you've done your job correctly in your design, this should only be done once per year.

You're also not going to make changes to the investment portfolio on a yearly basis due to lack of, or good, performance. You're not market timing; you're asset allocating.

CALENDAR QUARTER 1 MAINTENANCE

- ✓ RMD: If you're over 70, take your RMD. Did you take it from the most efficient place first? Take from equities you want to keep but are down, then cash? Did you use a cash or share distribution, and did you calculate before making the distribution?
- ✓ ROTH: Complete ROTH conversion analysis and move the most efficient assets from your IRA into your ROTH. If you did a ROTH conversion did you use a cash or a share distribution? If you used a share distribution, did you use shares at a loss strategy?
- ✓ Tax Allocation, Harvest, and Swaps: Review what capital assets you have in your retirement plans and which ordinary income assets you have in your non-IRA. Swap the assets to end up with the most tax efficient plan possible. If you have losses in a non-qualified account did you do a like kind harvest?

226

- ✓ HSA Analysis: Are you eligible? If so, fund this at the beginning of the year.
- ✓ Retirement Plan Contributions: Review your future allocations and determine if you should be adding to retirement plans with before-tax dollars. Or does it make more sense to add with after-tax dollars?
- ✓ Auto Insurance: PART I — Review your liability coverage and the deductibles. If you have the cash and/or credit available, then increase the deductible to reduce your premiums. PART II — Obtain bids to see if you can lower your costs.
- ✓ Homeowner's Insurance: PART I — Review your liability coverage and the deductibles. If you have the cash and/or credit available, then increase the deductible to reduce your premiums. PART II — Obtain bids to see if you can lower your costs.
- ✓ Umbrella Insurance: Review what coverage you have and look at your retirement plan within your online program. Determine what amount you have at risk.
- ✓ Life Insurance: Review the amount of cash value. What did it earn? Is there enough to pay the premiums and allow you to invest elsewhere? Do you have any debts that you are paying a higher interest on than the insurance is earning? Can you borrow from the life insurance to pay off those debts? Obtain bids from

brokers to see if you can lower the cost of the insurance.

✓ Disability: Review the amount of the coverage as it pertains to the amount of income you now earn. Do you need to increase it or decrease it? If the disability has a cap as a percentage of earnings and your earnings have gone down, then you have to reduce the policy. If you're nearing retirement, does the disability have a conversion to long-term care feature so you do not have to prove insurability?

✓ Long-Term Care Insurance: Review the amount. Did the coverage go up due to a COLA that is fixed? Or, if it's tied to the CPI, did the CPI go up? Is the coverage sufficient? Bid out the coverage with brokers to see if there's any way to reduce the costs. Review the waiting period and match that with the available assets to see if you should extend the waiting period to reduce the premiums.

✓ Cash Flow: Set your cash flow for the year. Determine the most tax efficient and risk efficient places to take the cash flow from for the next year.

✓ Asset Allocation Model: Based on your spending, your health and your goals, is the asset allocation model appropriate? DO NOT BASE THIS UPON YOUR EMOTION IN REGARDS TO THE MARKETS OR

ECONOMY. You should have already had your asset allocation model in place based on your original planning. If the model is not appropriate based on other factors, what do you have to do to change it?

✓ Asset Allocation: Rebalance — review your asset allocation model to determine what categories are out of balance. Rebalance if a category is out of tolerance by greater than 15%.

✓ Taxes: Have you paid enough in taxes for the prior year — by Jan 15th?

CALENDAR QUARTER 2 MAINTENANCE

✓ Tax Swapping: Are there investments you can swap between the before-tax and the after-tax accounts to show a paper loss but still keep the investment models intact?

✓ Beneficiary Check: Have you confirmed all beneficiary forms are correct, and you have physical copies of the forms confirming who is a beneficiary?

✓ Title/Deed Check: Have you confirmed all accounts are titled in your family trust or are titled in the correct name? Do you have physical proof?

✓ Quarterly Taxes: Have you paid your quarterly taxes to account for your new cash flow and possible capital gains?

✓ Cash Flow Check-In: Review how much you've spent

and compare to the original plan you set in place in Quarter 1. If you set your plan up automatically, this will be done for you and you simply need to review the analysis. You will spot trends and places that you might not have expected you would spend money in.
- ✓ If you're using a retirement corporation or LLC with a profit sharing plan, now is the time to complete your contributions.

CALENDAR QUARTER 3 MAINTENANCE
- ✓ Tax Swapping: Are there investments you can swap between the before-tax and the after-tax accounts to show a paper loss but still keep the investment models intact?
- ✓ Cash Flow Check-In: Review how much you have spent and compare to the original plan you set in place in Quarter 1. If you've set your plan up automatically, this will be done for you and you simply need to review the analysis. You will spot trends and places that you might not have expected you would spend money in.
- ✓ Quarterly Taxes: Have you completed your payment if necessary?

CALENDAR QUARTER 4 MAINTENANCE
- ✓ Tax Swapping: Are there investments you can swap between before-tax and the after-tax accounts to show a paper loss but still keep the investment models

intact? Keep wary of the 31-day wash rule. Use the not similar but unique strategy.

✓ Cash Flow Check-In: Review how much you've spent and compare to the original plan you set in place in. If you've set your plan up automatically, it will be done for you and you simply need to review the analysis. You'll spot trends and places you might not have expected you would spend money in.

✓ Quarterly Taxes: Have you paid your quarterly taxes to account for your new cash flow and possible capital gains?

✓ Tax Harvesting: Are any investments within your model down — ones that could be sold and repurchased into *similar but not the same* investments to book a paper loss?

These are the basic tasks on an annual basis. If you own a business, rental properties, or have special trusts like ILITs there are additional tasks needed.

There's a minimum of twenty-nine basic tasks every year.

The report card is more about creating a process. When completing it remember:

❖ You cannot control your investment returns.

❖ You can minimize and reduce risk, but you cannot control the returns.

❖ You can control your expenses, but you cannot

control interest rates.

- ❖ You can control your emotional actions, but you cannot control global economics.
- ❖ You can control investment expenses and what you get in value, but you cannot control taxes.
- ❖ You can minimize taxes, but you cannot control what happens globally.

Hopefully by now, you're equipped to assemble your TOTAL RETIREMENT FREEDOM plan.

You also now know the tools and the processes to maintain and run this beautiful machine called your financial business.

If you've gotten to this place and come to the conclusion this really is not for you, then read on. We'll explain how to find, hire, and work with someone to do all this for you.

If you're fairly confident that you'll handle this on your own, I wish you all the best on your road to YOUR TOTAL RETIREMENT FREEDOM PLAN. But if you're still uncertain, or you know you need to hire someone, let's head over to chapter 8.

CHAPTER 8

FINDING A FIDUCIARY ADVISOR

I'm assuming you've jumped ahead to this section because you've decided you want to work with someone to assist you in attaining your goals.

You might have worked with some type of advisor in the past, but have been disappointed. You might have even lost money working with someone.

Now I'll outline what you need to look out for and how to find, hire, and work with a pro.

To do this, it's important to understand the landscape of the financial industry.

DIFFERENCES BETWEEN FINANCIAL ADVISORS

I'm going to go back in history a bit to the place where I first started. You'll remember I started around 1984.

At that time there were only two types of financial people. There were stock brokers and insurance agents.

With the technology crash of 1999, the stock brokers had a credibility rating a notch below used car salesmen, but the financial companies are, and have always been, very smart.

Financial companies knew that the industry needed a

total perception makeover, so they changed the name to financial advisor from stock broker. This worked well for a number of years until all the recent scandals with big named financial advisors stealing billions of dollars of investors' money.

The term financial advisor took another credibility hit. The financial industry rebounded again by changing the name from financial advisor to wealth manager.

There are two sides to the financial industry, the Fiduciary side and the Broker side.

To make it even more confusing there are hybrids, people who operate on both sides of the game.

A financial advisor who works for themselves, or for a company, is either registered as a broker with FINRA or as a Fiduciary with the SEC.

If they're registered with the SEC, you'll usually see the acronym RIA. This means they're a Registered Investment Advisor. This is the sign that they are at least registered as a Fiduciary. It also means you have a full and transparent view through a federal disclosure called the form ADV Part II.

If they're registered as a broker, they work under the regulations called suitability. They can, and usually do, work in either their own company or a company's "best interest." They do not have a duty to do everything in your best interest.

If they work under the regulations as a fiduciary

(RIA), they owe you a duty of "best interest." Whatever they do, it MUST BE in your best interest, not theirs or their company's. They have more stringent oversight to be able to prove they are, in fact, doing everything in your best interest.

It gets even more confusing when you get an advisor who works for a FINRA broker and an SEC registered investment advisor.

These are referred to as Hybrid Advisors. You have to be very clear on each and every transaction, piece of advice, or interaction.

You have to ask whether there's a conflict of interest on every transaction because they're not required to disclose any conflicts as a broker.

If they're acting in this dual capacity, it would be like working with a doctor who makes commissions on some prescriptions. You would want to ask the doctor each time they prescribe something to you if there's a conflict of interest.

There has been much debate between the different sides within the financial industry.

In the early 2000s, the Financial Planning Association sued the SEC over the issue that brokers were calling themselves a "financial planner" and/or "financial advisor."

The reasoning was if you were a financial planner, you were taking on a fiduciary relationship with your client.

If you were a financial advisor or broker, you only had a suitability relationship.

Likewise, if you're a pediatrician, you can't advertise yourself as a brain surgeon.

Many brokerage companies had started calling themselves financial planners, wealth managers, or financial advisors.

This gave the public the impression the person helping you had a fiduciary duty to you like an RIA, CPA, or a lawyer.

It also gave the impression the person or company you're working with was looking at all aspects of your plan.

In my opinion, 90% of all financial companies care about one thing, getting your money into their accounts and funds.

The FPA ended up winning the lawsuit. I remember, I was in St. Petersburg Florida that day.

As I drove by a very large brokerage company, its sign read: "Come in to meet with a financial planner." I was not sure if they'd not gotten the word this was illegal, or they were just taunting the authorities to do something.

Here we are, years later, and this famed law (then called the Merrill Lynch Rule named after Merrill Lynch, which was one of the companies accused of using false names and titles) has since been overturned.

This could be why it's even harder for the public to really understand and know if whom you're dealing with has a fiduciary duty to you or not.

With this being said, I don't want you to believe that

just because you're dealing with a "true financial planner," you are protected.

I also don't want you to think if you're dealing with an "advisor" from a large Wall Street firm you're being ripped off.

It's best if you first understand the business models then you decide where you want to shop.

I would, however, suggest that if you're dealing with a large firm that has a dual role as broker and fiduciary, you get crystal-clear on what conflicts of interest are in your dealings.

Now let's discuss how different financial companies are organized and how they sell or dispense products and/or services to you.

Before I get into the real world details, let me help you understand it in another way.

When you and I go shopping, we go to one of four types of stores.

1) Corner store: 7-11, AM/PM, etc.
2) Mid-sized store: Albertsons, Vons, Publix, etc.
3) Superstores: Target, Walmart.
4) Specialty stores: Lowes, GNC, or Home Goods.

In the first three types of stores, you can buy the same name-brand gallon of dish detergent. The difference is the experience, the delivery system, and the price.

Let's first explore Option 1, the corner store.

When you go to a corner store, there's very limited

shelf space so you usually have a choice of one type of dish detergent.

It also may cost you $6.00 to buy that bottle of detergent.

Their business plan is they decide which dish detergent to put on their limited shelves space based on the profit margin they get from the distributor or manufacturer.

You also know when you go into these places it's convenient and fast. Not much has to be thought about because there's only one product to choose from.

Your next option is to go with the mid-sized store. This store might have four to six choices of dish detergent.

The nice part of this size store is you usually can find helpful people. The same gallon of dish detergent at this store might cost only $4.00.

Your last choice is to go to a Walmart or a Target. When you enter these places, the options are overwhelming.

You might now see ten or fifteen choices. If you need help finding out which dish detergent is best for you, have fun trying to find someone to help you at all.

In these "Big Box" stores, this same gallon of dish detergent might now cost you only $2.75. If you know exactly what you want and don't need any help, this is the place to go because it will save you money, if you can ever actually check out through the long lines.

Target isn't so bad but I still don't understand why every time I go into Walmart there are forty checkout lanes and only one is open with two hundred people waiting in line?

Each of these companies have a different business model. You should not get mad at the 7-11 and say they're "ripping you off" because that's what the 7-11 model is.

There's a benefit to being fast and not having to walk a marathon to get into the store.

Now let's talk about how these examples of companies relate to the same types of companies within the financial world.

Here's my disclosure to satisfy our legal department. That's right, you guys from legal, I know you're reading this and will put this in if I don't.

This discussion of financial institutions does not cover all the types, and is meant to be a general discussion. It's up to you to understand and ask questions of those you're dealing with. Hopefully, this book will arm you better. Here are the types of financial companies as they relate to the four types of retail models I just explained.

Corner Store.

This is the fast and convenient way to buy items. In the financial world, this would be companies that are large brokerage houses. In the past, these were usually identified as UBS, Merrill Lynch, Edward Jones, Raymond James, Morgan Stanley. Now you also have Wells Fargo Advisory and other banks with similar models.

239

When I talk about these companies, much of the confusion has come into place when the Glass-Steagall Act fell.

Now brokerage companies like UBS or Morgan Stanley have banking divisions.

Banks have brokerage divisions like Wells Fargo. While I did put these types of companies into the Corner Store category? Most of these large brokerage firms work on large volume and packaged products.

There are some very high level financial planners once you get to a very high net worth. Generally, that net worth starts at 10 million or more.

What I'm saying is that the consumer facing business model of most of these large companies is like the corner store.

As previously mentioned, when dealing with these companies you must also be very careful about conflicts of interest. The reason is that most of these companies are hybrids. They can act in both capacities of broker and fiduciary. You just have to know what, when, and how they are acting in every transaction.

When you enter these financial institutions, you'll usually meet with a financial advisor who has a compensation plan that is built on one thing and one thing only. It's to gather your assets into their institution and place them in what's called a packaged product.

Why packaged product?

A packaged product provides the client or consumer with little choice (remember the corner store?) and the maximum profitability to the company, (remember the corner store?).

These products usually fall into three categories:

1) Variable Annuities
2) Mutual Funds
3) Manager Wrap Programs

There are disadvantages and advantages with these packaged products.

The first advantage is that you have very few decisions to make. Most brokerage companies try to limit the choices both for inventory control and to make it easy for the consumer to make a quick decision.

For the beginning investor, or that investor who has less than $200,000, this might be a good alternative if you absolutely hate trying to figure out investments.

In my opinion and experience, these companies have a void in the expertise of distribution planning versus accumulation planning.

If you also understand that the broker or advisor gets paid on the amount they have in their accounts, you can also understand why it is not to their advantage to teach you how to take out a large income

These actions all reduce the amount they have in their accounts. The biggest disadvantage is the high costs you pay. (Need I mention the corner store again?) The three packaged products the brokerage firm sells are the highest cost investment programs on the market. Here are a few examples.

Variable Annuities.

These products put mutual funds inside an annuity wrapper. The selling points I've heard from brokers is that you don't pay taxes when you sell a fund and move it from one fund to another fund.

The TRUTH is you don't pay immediate taxation but when you take it out, you'll pay the tax.

If your variable annuity isn't in a retirement plan, you're losing the capital gain benefit that you would normally receive on a sale of an investment.

Inside of a variable annuity, you pay ordinary income taxes on any profits. This will actually increase taxation.

They will tell people there is a death benefit. TRUTH. The death benefit, in my opinion, is a sham. It usually says they'll pay out the higher of the highest anniversary value or the current cash value.
You'll pay for that death benefit but it will only pay off when the market crashes and you have to time your death to happen when the market is down.

If the market is up and you die, they do not pay any death benefit even though you've paid for the benefit. This is, in my opinion, a benefit too heavily weighted towards the insurance companies' benefit and against you.

Another way the salespeople sell this product is they tell people that, "You don't have to medically qualify for the death benefit." This is true, but now you know why.

They rarely pay out a net gain above the actual cash value. It's usually the same financial advisor trying to convince you to put more into the stock market, who will show you the chart of how the market is up four days to every one down day.

If this is the case, how can they justify selling a variable annuity on the death benefit factor when in fact they are having their customers pay the cost of insurance *and* there's only a one out of four chance the insurance company will have to pay anything?

Think about it this way: if they're promoting how great their funds are, the death benefit never really gets paid out.

If they're promoting how great the death benefit is, what they are really saying is that, on average, their funds will underperform the markets as you have a better chance of collecting on the death benefit than you do on the funds.

The TRUTH is the amount of the death benefit is only the difference between your actual cash value and the stated death benefit.

This means that if you invested $100,000 in a variable annuity and the market dropped to $90,000 they would only be responsible for $10,000.

The TRUTH is the death benefit is not tax-free like actual life insurance. Annuities do not have any tax-free benefits.

If you did in fact die when the market was down, the death benefit becomes taxable at the highest type of tax, ordinary income tax.

Funds within an annuity wrapper: Variable annuities have a menu of funds, very much like your 401-K.

Do you get a choice of picking which funds are in there? No! (Corner store again.)

The insurance company picks the available funds to go on the menu for you.

Just like a 401-K, a variable annuity isn't going to have the highest performing funds with the lowest fees in each category.

As a matter of fact, the funds in a variable annuity are not the same funds which have the same name as you are used to.

Take the Fidelity Magellan Fund. You can go to the open market and buy the real Fidelity Magellan Fund. When you buy it through a variable annuity, it's under the same name, but it's not the same fund.

It cannot own the same exact investments in the same percentages because this fund was created just for this

244

insurance company and just this variable annuity product.

In many cases the fund manager may even be different as they may be a sub-manager. It's all about the branding and the name perception.

You can imagine what happens when clients come in and wonder why the variable annuity their broker sold them does not have the same tracked performance the fund listed in the paper or on the Internet has.

Variable Annuity Fees. This is where I think I have my biggest issue with variable annuities. Most variable annuities have fees between 2% and 4%.

This is outrageous considering the first 2%-4% of returns goes to the investment advisor, the brokerage company and the insurance company, for doing what long term?

These fees add up between the mortality and expense (M&E), the rider fees and then the hidden fees that a mutual fund charges are added on.

In summary, there are very few investment programs I try to keep clients out of. This is due to my belief every tool has a place in the toolbox. This is one of those products we try to make sure we generally keep clients out of.

I've mentioned a few times before that there are always exceptions and nothing is absolute.

If I find a client who is in need of life insurance, yet is uninsurable, there are two companies offering liquid and low-cost variable annuities, Fidelity and Vanguard. This is a unique and remote option but sometimes it is needed.

Mutual Funds.

Mutual funds are usually sold by brokerage firms because they're popular. Popularized by 401-Ks, they've become the most acceptable investment method.

Unfortunately, doctors in the 1940s told people it was healthy and good for them to smoke. Here we are sixty years later and now we really know.

It still doesn't stop everyone from smoking but you better believe they know it is killing them.

I have the same opinion about open-ended mutual funds.

In the early 1980s, when I first started, there were only about 600 mutual funds available. Now, as of this writing, there are over 31,000 mutual funds.

They wouldn't proliferate so fast if they weren't incredibly profitable to those who issue and sell them.

Much of their profits are in the form of hidden fees.

How do open-ended mutual funds work? There are different types or class shares of mutual funds.

Front Load Funds, otherwise known as an A Class Funds are one only a type of open ended fund. They charge anywhere between 3% and 6% to buy in.

This means you're only working with 94% to 97% of your original investment dollars. You have to catch up before you can get ahead. In addition, these funds carry management fees, potential 12-B1 fees and non-disclosed trading fees.

Back-End Load, otherwise known as a B Class Fund are another type of open ended fund. They don't charge you anything up front but if you cash out of the fund within a prescribed period of time, you'll pay the load or fee.

You have to watch these funds, because instead of charging you a one-time upfront fee, they increase the management fee.

Over time, they not only collect what the A Class Fund would have collected but sometimes it actually costs you much more.

C Class Funds are the last type of open-ended fund. These funds have no buy-in costs, but they usually add an additional fee onto the already high management fee.

An example would be a Class A fund might charge you 2% in annual management fees, whereas a Class C fund share would charge you 3%. If you add this up over time, it can be a small fortune.

No-Load Fund. There's really no such thing. The reason there's no such thing as a no-load fund is there are operating costs.

There will always be operating costs. So NO, there will never be any such thing as a true "no-load."

The broker or advisor will argue back and say, "We were only referring to whether the fund had an upfront fee or not."

I'm not one for that excuse as the general public does

not know (and probably does not want to know) about the difference between a front-end fee, a management fee, a 12-B1 fee, or trading fees.

The bottom line is that some "no-load" funds have higher ownership costs than those you pay a front-end load to. In either case, there's a cost.

The reason the corner-store-brokerage type company uses these packaged products are they're easy to explain, involve little choice and have high profits.

Mutual funds also market their funds just like any other product, by branding them.

Large mutual funds like Franklin, Fidelity, or Vanguard are common names so people feel comfortable with them. This branding has nothing to do with whether the funds have high fees or comparable performance to their peers or the indexes. People get used to a name, they trust it, and they buy it based on that.

Most people have no idea who their manager is of their mutual fund, what their track record is, or what their actual returns, risks, or fees are.

It's my opinion the reason the corner store brokerage type companies use this product is it's very profitable.

If they sell a fund and collect 5% up front and then another 1% each year, they can afford the leaded glass chandeliers, the cherry wood desks, the marble floors in their offices, and the Bentleys in the parking spaces.

The other big reason the corner store type brokerage

firms use mutual funds is there's literally nothing for the brokerage firm to manage.

The mutual funds themselves are the ones who manage your money.

The mutual fund manager is the one who does the buying and selling and is responsible for your account.

Wrap Accounts.

This is the newest invention from the brokerage industry. Each company may brand it with their own name, but here's the simple concept.

The brokerage company will take either no-load mutual funds and/or independent investment managers and bring them into their wrap program.

Under their wrap program, you have the choice of different mutual funds or managers in each category. While I like this concept because it allows different asset allocation categories to be represented, there can be some real problems.

A) Wrap programs are not tax sensitive. They will move money between managers and when this is done it can create a tax gain or loss.

B) Wrap programs are very expensive for just money management. If you take a no-load fund that might be charging you 2% in management fees and then you add on the brokerage company's 1% to 1.5% in management fees, you're topping 2%-3% in fees. This is not much different than the variable annuity problem.

Hopefully you now better understand what I call the corner store financial advisor model.

Superstores.

The second type of model compares to Walmart. This is where you'll find the retail stores or online stores like Scottrade, E*TRADE, Fidelity, and Charles Schwab.

They'll usually have offices in which you can go visit. They can offer you just about any investment available. While this is better than the limits the corner store model imposes, it's now overwhelming on what to choose from.

Unfortunately, these investment stores are not housed with people who are fiduciary advisors.

They're usually not allowed to dispense investment, tax, trust or financial planning advice. They can pull an investment prospectus and explain how an investment works, but cannot tell you if it's right for you or not.

They cannot create comprehensive tax, trust, and investment coordinated financial plans.

They're sometimes referred to as discount brokers. The prices are super cheap and sometimes no cost.

This is where someone would go if they were putting their own plan together and really knew their way around the financial world.

Specialty Stores

Just like going into a GNC, you have to really know what you are looking for and you better read the label. The people working in GNCs are not nutritionists. While they might tell you about a new supplement or try to push you towards a special, they don't understand the interactions of the ingredients in each vitamin or supplement like a nutritionist would.

Now imagine you have a personal shopper. This shopper knows you, what you want, what you need, and what you must stay away from. How do they know that?

They've spent time to understand you, your goals, your needs, and things you might be allergic to.

You hire that person to go to the large big box stores and sometimes even the specialty stores. They pick out the items for you which will fit into your overall plan.

They don't earn a commission on items they pick out; rather you pay them to work in your best interest, like a nutritionist.

This is a Fiduciary Advisor/Planner. You'll find that they will usually use a discount broker such as Schwab, TD Ameritrade, or Fidelity.

They'll usually work on the institutional side rather than the retail side. (When you enter a retail store/office for Fidelity, Schwab or TD Ameritrade, you're working on the retail side - which is not a Fiduciary Advisor/Planner).

HOW TO FIND THE RIGHT PERSON

Much has been written about, talked about, and argued about on how to find the right person.

I don't have the perfect answer for you. All I can tell you is that every source comes with its own problems. The main ways to find the right person are:

1) Referral from family or friend.

I'm not sold on this idea as most people would think. What if the person you're getting referred by has absolutely no idea how the advisor works but just likes them? I now call this the Madoff factor. Bernie Madoff's clients were referred to him by current investors, investors who told their friends, family and neighbors to invest with him, because they liked him and he made them money.

While you need to like the person you're working with it should only be 10% - 20% of the total decision. Your future is at stake and you must have the most qualified person steering your ship through the dangerous and choppy waters called retirement.

2) Use the Internet. You could start calling and trying to find the right person by the Internet (the new Yellow Pages).

Again, you have no idea what or who these people might be. There are a lot of connection services out there that have a referral service.

You input what you want and it will narrow down the list of people for you.

I'm not 100% sold on this idea of how to do it because I've heard the horror stories from current clients, before they became my clients.

The stories are the same as those from people who have tried to use the online dating services.

In many cases, there's a picture of a gorgeous person, but once you meet them, you wonder when that online picture was taken or maybe they just aged twenty years in a week.

If you're going to use this method of finding a professional, then please do your homework to really investigate the advisor.

3) CPA or Lawyer. My best and most collaborative relationships come from these types of relationships. These sources are centers of influence that usually don't refer me clients who would not be good clients to work with.

On the other hand, a CPA or lawyer may or may not have a good understanding of what's right and fair. I've had situations where the CPA or lawyer is referring someone to a full-charge broker because they're just not aware. We've also seen cases where a lawyer is referring a client to a broker with whom he plays golf with or the advisor is buying him a vacation each year.

There should be a clear and respectable reason as to why the CPA or lawyer is making the referral, so ask them.

You're being provided with the information within this book to be able to know what questions to ask but you have to do the work and ask for proof.

I originally stated that it should be a combination of

experience, specialized knowledge, a love for what they do, the value they provide for the fee they charge and will they be able to get you to your goals.

Like a good CEO, watch out for who you bring into your team. Also ask the advisor for their net worth, their investment, or guaranteed annual income. If they're not able to show you how they've done it for themselves, how will they be able to do it for you?

COMPARING FEES AND VALUES OF OUTSOURCING YOUR FINANCIAL WORK

There's been much debate on fees and who's high and who is low. I'm going to make sense of this for you from a purely "Service Provided" standpoint.

Fees are generally broken into four actual categories: Number five is something you would never worry about with a fiduciary only advisor.

- ❖ **Initial planning fees.**
- ❖ **Ongoing management fees.**
- ❖ **Commissions.**
- ❖ **Hourly fees.**
- ❖ **Hidden fees.**

If you remember, there are two different types of financial people, those who act in a fiduciary capacity and those who do not.

Is it possible to have someone act in a dual capacity? The answer is yes and we will address that, too.

Here is a simple outline of how each one gets paid.

Hourly

Fiduciary Advisor
This is a normal way to charge. Not much different than your CPA or Lawyer.

Non-Fiduciary Advisor or Broker
May not charge any hourly fee.

On Going Management Fees

Fiduciary Advisor
This is a normal way to charge. Not much different than hiring your CPA to run your business or do your financials or audits or having a lawyer on retainer.

Non-Fiduciary Advisor or Broker
May not charge an ongoing fee.

<u>Initial Planning Fees</u>

Fiduciary Advisor
This is like hiring an architect to have blueprints drafted.
You always want to see if you're free to build your plan with
anyone you want, or whether the planner owns the rights to
the plan and you can only implement it through them.

Non-Fiduciary Advisor or Broker
May not charge any fee of any type, either for plan design or
creation.

<u>Commission</u>

Fiduciary Advisor
Maybe, If the advisor or firm has a dual registration they
might be able to get paid on certain types of business.

Non-Fiduciary Advisor or Broker
This is the only way that **<u>a non-fiduciary</u>** advisor may get
paid.

Now, hopefully. you understand the different ways to
compensate someone you will work with.

Should you pay commissions, management fees or
hourly fees to this person?

For over thirty years, I've always stayed in the middle

256

of this argument. I've heard from colleagues on the commission side tell me this always best serves the client.

On the fee only side, I hear my colleagues tell me the commission guys are always ripping people off.

I don't hold judgment on either side but only look at the calculations.

If I go to a brokerage house and they recommend that I buy a group of mutual funds, pay a load, and then have them manage it, I'll look at the total fees.
Here is an example:

$500,000 invested at a 5.75% front load costs me $28,750.00 in front-end commissions.

These are fees that are taken out before my money gets invested. After the brokerage company takes out their fee then I have $471,250 left to invest out of my original $500,000.

Assuming the mutual fund falls into the average domestic equity fee range, it will cost me 1.5% in mutual fund management fees.

Further assuming I'm using a domestic equity fund with an average annual turnover of 50%, it will cost me another 1%-2% in transaction costs. I will not see these charges as they're deducted at the fund level, not on my monthly statement.

If this hasn't been painful enough, then add on a tax cost. If my money is invested in a non-qualified account, then I may have a tax due.

This tax is because the Tax Code treats mutual funds unfairly. If the manager creates a realized gain, then you have to pay taxes on it even if the fund has lost value. The estimate is that if the fund has a 50% turnover this will cause another tax equal to .50%

If you added these all up it is tremendous:

Front Load Commissions	$28,750
Annual Operating Expense	$14,137
Tax Cost (Taxable distribution x 30% tax bracket)	$ 7,068
Total Cost First Year	$49,955 (9.99%)
Annual Ongoing Cost	$21,205 (4.49%)

Note: You're getting the mutual fund, or funds to do one thing: manage the money. You're not getting someone to oversee your overall investment allocation, your tax plan, your estate plan, your asset protection plan, and your insurance risk plan.

Now let's take another example. I go to a financial planner. I pay him/her an average of $2,500 in an initial planning fee (these fees range from $1,500 to $25,000 depending on your estate, tax and overall financial complications) to outline my entire future.

I get an investment plan, a tax plan, an estate plan, an asset protection plan, and insurance risk plan.

Once the plan is complete, the planner finds independent money managers who do not charge an upfront fee, commission, or load.

This would be through ETFs, closed-end funds, professional money managers, or a selected stock or bond basket.

The planner helps you select the investments that have the best-in-class performance, fees structure, and risk. Most important, the selection is to fit the right investments into your tax and cash flow plan.

For planning comparisons, let's assume your total investment is still $500,000. Now let's look at the numbers together.

Initial planning fees. $2,500

Investment Management
(No load to use these investments)
½ Percent for professional
manager and or ETF fee = $2,500
1.% for ongoing tax, allocation
and oversight management by
the financial planner. $5,000

<u>Total cost of first year</u> $10,000

Ongoing cost of Year two
and beyond $7,500
As a percentage of portfolio   (1.5%)

<u>First Year Comparison</u>

Mutual Fund Model $49,995
(does not include a plan)

Cost of Fiduciary Model $10,000
(includes a plan)

Difference in dollars

$39,995

Difference in percentage
for first year   7.99%

<u>Ongoing</u>

Cost of Mutual Fund Model $21,205
(Does not include ongoing
Financial, tax, estate or insurance
 Planning)

Cost of Fiduciary Model $7,500

(Includes total financial
oversight and automated tracking)
Difference in dollars $13,705

Difference in a percentage
for ongoing costs   2.99%

What difference does this have over a period of time?
    If we compared these two models over a period of ten
years at the same rate of return of 8%, the results are
staggering.
In the Mutual Fund Model,
you start off with   -------------------->$500,000
but at the end of ten years
you end up with ————————->$677,366.

    In the Fiduciary Model we will even take the
beginning point down by the upfront fee paid for a full
financial plan.
    This is not a fair comparison since when you buy a
mutual fund you don't get a plan.
    For the purposes of this comparison I will deduct the
fee just to show you how, even after you pay a fee for a plan,
you are still much further ahead.
If we start off with the
same exact amount of ----------------->$500,000
in ten years, under the

same rate of return the
Fiduciary Model has --------------------->$938,952 dollars.

That's right, you are ahead by --------->$261,586.

Earlier I spoke about some other books that teach you that you can get ahead by saving a few bucks a week by not drinking coffee or a coke.

If you research these same authors they're from brokerage houses that sell the mutual fund models.

Of course you have to stop drinking coffee; that money has to go to pay the brokers, the brokerage houses and the mutual fund companies.

If you want a real boost to your wealth, then understand where the big fees are and reduce your non-value costs.

If mutual funds consistently underperform the markets and overcharge for it, are you getting value? If you are paying a large fee each year, are you getting a total financial plan or just someone who

> "It's it is not what something costs but what value you get from it."
> **Warren Buffett**

is buying and selling investments?

Wow, that was eye opener, right? This goes back to the discussion on what type of store you will shop at.

Are you going to go to the corner store or the

Walmart/Target?

PREPARING FOR YOUR FIRST MEETING

At this point, you should have completed the following tasks:

1. Completed your goals worksheets to understand what you want.
2. Assembled all your financial and estate planning documents.
3. Researched and found at least three planners or advisors you'll be sending a preliminary questionnaire to.

The next step is to send out a preliminary questionnaire to understand how the advisor works and what you can expect.

If the advisor is a top advisor or planner, they'll also have a preliminary questionnaire they'll send you.

Most top advisors I know are very selective and will not take anyone as a client, no matter how much money they might have.

If you'd like to see what a client preliminary questionnaire looks like, you can go to:
www.Kenhimmler.com/trf/cfq

For your questionnaire you want to make sure you ask the following questions of your potential candidate:
Who they are. Ask for their personal background.

➢   Who do they work for now and who have they worked for?

➢   How they are compensated? Fiduciary, broker, or both?

➢   What services do I get for the fee?

➢   Are there any other charges?

➢   Are there connected services such as legal, tax, insurance, and if so, how does the coordination work? Differentiate between them knowing someone to refer you to versus a team in-house.

➢   Review of their communications policy and who would do what. (A communications policy is a written format of who you work with, how do you communicate and what their turnaround time is in getting back to you.) This prevents the situation where you think you're working with one person but then get handed off to someone else.

➢   If they're a Fiduciary, a review of their ADV Part II and Firm Brochure.

➢   What is their process initially?

➢   What is their process ongoing?

➢   Who do they specialize with?

➢   What is their criteria for being accepted as a client? If they don't do both a financial and a personality qualification, then they probably accept anyone. You may run into problems in the future as they may only care about taking in new clients, not serving the ones they have.

➢   What actions would be cause to let   client go? If

264

they don't have this outlined, I would be very wary. It should be clear as to the type of person they want to deal with. It should also be clear as to why you as a client might be let go.

➢ What continuity plan do they have in place in case of disaster?

➢ If all of your documents, taxes, insurances, and financial plans are with one person, do they have protections and steps in place to protect you? This would also include death, disability, or retirement of the person you are working with.

➢ Are there resources to learn what strategies they use?

➢ Are they growth-minded investors, contrarian, or value style investors? Do they use market timing, otherwise known as tactical strategies, or do they use strategic asset allocation? If you have not decided on what type of investor you are, you might be asking for trouble hiring someone who does things you do not understand, or that you don't agree with.

➢ How many clients does the person you're dealing with handle? Each advisor or direct person you deal with should not be working with more than 75 clients. We know that is the maximum even with the best tools. When the advisor is truly working on all the tasks we listed under Calendar Quarter Maintenance, this should be the maximum number of clients to be responsible for.

➢ On average, how much time and how many meetings will the planner be working with you on? Will this changeover time? I know in our practice, the first year we spend about fifty to sixty hours meeting with and working on a new client's plan. In the second and subsequent years it drops to forty hours a year or ten hours a quarter. This is because it takes us a long time to get everything on track. Once we get everything fixed, our technology oversees the direction of the plan. The technology tells us when someone gets off track so we can look into it. If the plan is set up correctly, the ongoing management is much easier, assuming there are automation tools in place.

➢ Is there an automated system in place to oversee my plan and what are the costs? I believe this is the most important question. If you're working with a planner who has more than ten clients, there's no way they can be watching your investments, taxes, insurances, trusts, and overall financial plan on a daily basis. This is where the technology and automation come into play. These tools are very expensive, which is why many planners choose to set up plans but do not monitor them full-time. It's important to know if you're hiring a full-time manager or just someone who will draw the plan up and only look at it occasionally.

I would suggest you initially do the interview by phone or send the questionnaire by email or mail. This way, you can leave the human emotion out of the equation. Ask them to return the questionnaire at least a week in advance of your first appointment.

Assuming you have done a good job and are about 90% confident this person is the one you want to work with,

266

the next step is to put together your data and prepare for the first meeting.

This meeting can be in person or by phone. I would always suggest to not let distance limit the talent you want to work for you.

If you find someone that can do this job for you then hire them no matter where they are. About 50% of my clients are in different cities or countries. I have clients on four continents and never met 20% of them.

With phone, internet, email, and scanning, distance should not be a limiting factor. Don't let distance limit the talent you can hire.

DATA

Your data falls into two categories. The first and most important are your goals. If you've not already downloaded the goals sheet you can go to www.kenhimmler.com/trf/goals

The second important task is to complete a quantitative worksheet. This will list all of your information that your person will need in order to complete a comprehensive analysis.

You can also download this worksheet by going to www.kenhimmler.com/trf/CFQ

Another option is you can put all your data into MoneyGuidePro first. Once it's in the program, you can print out a very organized data report that you can give to your planner. This would include your goals, your income and expenses, and all your assets and liabilities. Once you have completed both of these worksheets you're now prepared for your first meeting.

YOUR FIRST MEETING

We will assume that you're meeting with a top end planner. Any top planner is going to be very hard to get to and will have many rules on whom they do not accept as clients.

To help you prepare, I might start off by telling you about the cases that I do and don't take.

I've taken smaller size cases if the person is nice, needs my help, and will not be a burden.

When I say smaller cases, I mean cases in which there is less than $2,000,000 to work with.

It has nothing to do with the amount we earn, but I have learned that the lower the net worth, the more work, time, and explaining it takes from us.

We can work with someone who has $50,000,000 and the amount of time it takes us is usually 25% of the time it takes us when we work with someone that has $500,000.

The reason is the high net worth person already understands much of what we do, they make quick and decisive decisions and they also are great collaborators.

The one piece of wisdom I have learned from super high net worth people is they never say, "I already know," or "I won't do that because someone told me such and such."

The super high net worth person looks at it like a business (usually because they obtained their money through applying the same process in a business).

Here are the reasons why we don't take someone on, or will let a client go:

1) A person who is not forthcoming about all their finances. As a fiduciary, we have a liability and responsibility for recommendations which require us to see the whole picture.

2) A person who thinks they already know it all. This is called financial arrogance. We generally see many mistakes these people are making which cost them a lot of money.

Unfortunately, they have a confidence problem or an insecurity that requires them to beat their own drum. Any successful advisor does not have time for this.

3) If a couple is married, the one who handles the finances has to show off for the other spouse or defend mistakes made.

It's like working in a company. If one person cannot look at what is trying to be accomplished and simply move on, it holds up the entire process and team.

4) Rumors, hearsay, or popular opinion. If someone comes in telling us about how they "read on the Internet," or they knew someone that did this or that and it did not work out, we will not want to work with them.

Any top-end planner will be working with facts, under current rules and conditions, and will be measuring if a strategy is good for the client at that time.

Whatever someone's neighbor's brother's friend in Michigan did twenty years ago that did not work, does not apply in a calculation and professional business environment. 5) Not caring about others they're responsible for. This is one criteria that I've added because of my personal values. It's not one that may be a rule breaker for your planner but it is for me. This is when one spouse does not care what happens to the other one.

It may be when we find the main decision maker is taking too much risk. They don't have any or enough coverage for life or long-term care when needed. They may not have a trust or a current updated plan for their spouse's protection.

In these cases, when the client says, "Let them fend for themselves," we'll find another planner at another firm for that client. The client is not always that brash in words but the intent is there.

6) When a client doesn't pay their bills to us on time. This is a mutual respect issue.

When we are on time with our deliverables and always concerned about getting our clients to their goals, the client should pay their bills on time.

This is a fair exchange for both. If you hire a planner that is working for you and helping you get to your goals, be willing and prompt in their payment, trust me, they'll have you on their minds.

7) When a prospective client only wants to give us a little

piece to manage, this is better suited for a money manager, not a comprehensive planner.

Any top-end planner is not interested in managing a piece of money because it may conflict with other parts of the client's plan and hurt them more then help them.

This is why a doctor asks for all prescriptions you're taking or if you're allergic to anything. A caring doctor doesn't want to hurt you.

8) Not taking the advice given. I don't know of any of my colleagues who expect every client to follow every piece of advice given.

I do know that all top planners look at when a piece of advice is given and if it is not followed, how it affects other parts of the plan.

As an example, if a planner gives a strategy recommendation on how to reduce income tax and it's not followed, and the client complains they're paying too much tax, a decision is usually made whether to keep or let that client go.

The decision to keep or let the client go is based on whether the client is really in a partnership with the planner or not.

9) How nice and courteous they are to staff. We have let clients go because they're nasty to the team, and the minute they get on the phone with me they're nice as pie.

In any top planning office, there's a team that takes care of the client. They all deserve to be treated with respect as they're the ones assisting in getting the client to their goal.

These are our primary reasons why we might not take on a client or might let a client go. You'll have to ask the advisor candidate you're interviewing what their criteria might be.

To make sure you are not blindsided with a termination letter, ask the planner if they'll give notice to you of at least thirty days if they decide to let you go.

Also, ask if they have a board that makes decisions on letting a client go or not. If they have a board and the board decides to let a client go, ask what the appeal process is.

We have a board that meets on a quarterly basis. We review those clients we feel are not in a partnership with us. If we feel as though it's in the firm's and the client's best interest to part, we have a discussion with the client.

If the client disagrees with the reasons, and we cannot come to a compromise, we do everything we can to help them find another firm.

If the client is unreasonable, we do not refer to them to any colleagues or other firms we respect.

We don't want to be known as the firm that sends our fired clients to a respected firm which we may be working with in the future.

With those items in mind now, you should be ready to meet with your potential candidate for the first time.

CHAPTER 9 .... HOW TO WORK
WITH A PLANNER

Assuming you have found the right person to work with, I can tell you there's one secret to working with your planner and your plan – and it is:

COMMUNICATION

Communication is the number one quality that makes a sound working partnership.

Good communication is when a client provides us the clearest understanding of what they want, how they want it, and when they want it.

It also includes the conditions on how they want to get to their goals. When this is done, they're the easiest clients to create plans and implement plans for.

The hardest clients to create plans for are the ones who have a lot of confusion as to what they want, and let outside noise like friends, family, fears, and news get in the way.

When you're working with your planner and they come up with ideas and strategies on how to get you to your goals, ask them the most important questions.

➤ **What is the risk?**
➤ **What is the cost?**

- ➢ **Can I make changes along the way?**
- ➢ **If this does not work, what are my alternatives?**
- ➢ **What are the benefits?**
- ➢ **What are the downsides?**

A lot of times, clients will want to know how something internally works.

In many cases, it's so in-depth the client would not understand even if the explanation was detailed.

Let's assume you went to the doctor. He recommends an X-Ray.

It would not help to ask the doctor explain where the X-Ray machine is manufactured or how it works.

You would have to have a deep education in electrical engineering, radiology, and manufacturing.

In the end, that information is not going to help you, nor is it the doctor's job to educate someone one this. What *will* help you is knowing:

- ➢ **What is the risk?**
- ➢ **What is the cost?**
- ➢ **Can I make changes along the way?**
- ➢ **If this does not work, what are my alternatives?**
- ➢ **What are the benefits?**
- ➢ **What are the downsides?**

Not a typo, yes I repeated that list above and broke every editing rule out there. If you read it again it'll make it all worth breaking the rules!

IMPLEMENTING YOUR PLAN

If you took the time to read the chapters on how to implement a plan (under the do it yourself section – **Chapter 7**), then you should already know the steps.

CREATING A SCHEDULE FOR ONGOING MANAGEMENT

Here is the wonderful thing about hiring someone else, you don't have a lot to do.
Your goal is the CEO. Here are your tasks:

1) Provide a clear and understandable vision of who you are and what you want.
2) Provide a clear and defined list of goals with dates and dollar amounts.
3) Provide details on all financial facts such as assets, liabilities, income, expenses and insurances.
4) Provide the details on conditions of getting to your goals. Things you do and don't like.
5) Review annually your progress and make adjustments as needed.
6) Provide any changes throughout the year that may send your plan of course.

ADVISOR REPORT CARD

Using a report card for an advisor is important. It will lay out your expectations and it will help you understand if the person or firm is meeting, exceeding, or failing your expectations.

Like hiring an employee, you must outline your expectations. If you get upset at your advisor for missing an expectation, you must firstly ask:

1) Was this expectation clearly outlined?

2) Was there a mutual agreement to achieve this expectation?

3) Is there an expectation impossible for the advisor to achieve? As an example, if you cannot control the interest rates, markets, or volatility, then how can you expect an advisor to control it? You can use the list of the items from Chapter 3, what you can and cannot control.

Here's a sample report card you can use for an advisor: This should be done at least annually but no more frequent than semi-annually.

If you would like a fillable version of this report card, you can go to kenhimmler.com/trf/reportcard

Question 1
Have I had a detailed discussion with my planner on my income taxes and different methods on how to reduce my liability?
Grade A, B, C, D

Question 2
Has my planner shown me my future cash value, income, and expense projections and helped me understand what I can spend without running out of money?
Grade A, B, C, D

Question 3
Has my volatility risk been fully explained and do I understand how this affects my plan?
Grade A, B, C, D

Question 4
Do I have a distribution plan in place that will give me the most efficient distribution based on my plans?
Grade A, B, C, D

Question 5
Has my advisor gone through all the stress tests with me so I know where my family would be in case of catastrophe from premature death?
Grade A, B, C, D

Question 6
Has my family trust and estate plan been reviewed and updated this year?
Grade A, B, C, D

Question 7
Has the family trust distribution flow been reviewed and explained to me?
Grade A, B, C, D

Question 8
Has my insurance been reviewed and compared?
Grade A, B, C, D

Question 9
Has the asset allocation model been reviewed with me and agreed upon, based on my needed income and cash flows?
Grade A, B, C, D

Question 10
Do I have an open line of communications with not only my planner/advisor but also with the team that supports them?
Grade A, B, C, D

Question 11

Have we had an overall discussion on my goals and how my plan is progressing towards my goals?

Grade A, B, C, D

Question 12
Based on my risk and the categories invested in, how have my investments performed compared to an identical benchmark?

Grade A, B, C, D

The asset allocation model will determine the rate of return over a period of time.

That period of time is different for everyone, based on your individual financial plan.

If you and your planner have done the job correctly, the asset allocation model is synchronized with your plan.

You will find the discussion on whether the volatility is being correctly discussed with you as a grade, as that is something that can be semi-controlled by the asset allocation model. This is why there is a grade for this.

If you do not like the volatility, then your planner/advisor should be discussing with you either alternative allocation models or the ways to insure the model you do have against excessive volatility.

After you have graded the review, then you should meet with your planner to review the strong and weak points. Have a discussion on how you can improve what your expectations are.

Conclusion

Congratulations! You've made it to the end of your plan. At this point, you should either have your plan in place by doing it yourself, or you should have found someone to do it for you.

In either case, you are now in the 10% of people who create a plan and follow through with it.

Like a diet in which you lost 30 pounds, the key now is to keep it off. In planning terms, it means to keep up your plan. It makes more sense to keep up your plan than to let it go, and having to start again from the beginning every five years.

For continuing education, please visit our site at www.kenhimmler.com/trf

Made in the USA
San Bernardino, CA
28 July 2016